Malaria and the DDT Story

Malaria and the DDT Story

RICHARD TREN
ROGER BATE

The Institute of Economic Affairs

First published in Great Britain in 2001 by
The Institute of Economic Affairs
2 Lord North Street
Westminster
London SW1P 3LB
in association with Profile Books Ltd

A CIP catalogue record for this book is available from the British Library.

ISBN 0 255 36499 7

Many IEA publications are translated into languages other than English or are
reprinted. Permission to translate or to reprint should be sought from the
General Director at the address above.

Typeset in Stone by MacGuru
info@macguru.org.uk

Printed and bound in Great Britain by Hobbs the Printers

CONTENTS

The authors   7

Foreword by Harold M. Koenig   9

Summary   13

List of tables   15

1   **Introduction**   19

2   **Historical malaria control policies**   21
    Environmental vector control   22
    Chemical vector control   25

3   **Drug therapy against malaria**   28
    Historic drug policies   28
    Current drug policies   30
    Vaccine   33

4   **DDT and the global eradication campaign**   35
    Plus ça change – past and present malaria
        control policies   41

5   **Environmentalism and malaria control**   45
    Donor agencies, malaria control and environmentalism   49
    Environmentalism and disease control   53

Environmental folly   59
The precautionary principle and DDT   59
Sustainability for whom?   61

6   **DDT – environmental saviour?**   65
    Pesticide resistance and the case for DDT   68

7   **Economic cost of malaria**   74
    Government regeneration and the control of malaria   75
    Malaria and Mozal – doing good while doing well   75
    Data collection initiative   78
    Mozal malaria costs (indirect)   79
    Mozal malaria costs (direct)   80
    Mozal vector control   82
    Opportunity costs of malaria   85

8   **Wider economic costs**   87

9   **Conclusion**   91

    References   95

    About the IEA   106

THE AUTHORS

Roger Bate

Roger Bate is Media and Development Director for the International Policy Network and a fellow of the Institute of Economic Affairs. He founded the Environment Unit at the Institute of Economic Affairs in 1993 and co-founded the European Science and Environment Forum in 1994.

Dr Bate has several degrees including a PhD in economics from the University of Cambridge and an MSc in Environmental and Resource Economics from University College, London. He recently completed a research project for the South African government's Water Research Commission and he also advised on several Masters students' theses.

Dr Bate is the editor of *What Risk?* (Butterworth Heinemann, 1997), a collection of papers that critically assess the way risk is regulated in society. He has also written several scholarly papers and numerous shorter scientific articles for newspapers and magazines including the *Wall Street Journal, British Medical Journal, Financial Times, Business Standard, Financial Express, San Francisco Examiner, Los Angeles Times* and *Accountancy*. His most recent book is *Life's Adventure: Virtual Risk in a Real World* (Butterworth Heinemann, 2000).

Richard Tren

Richard Tren is a South African, but he received most of his education in the UK. He has an honours degree in economics from St Andrews University in Scotland and an MSc in Environmental and Resource Economics from University College, London. He returned to South Africa in 1997 after studying and working in Europe for almost ten years. He works as a consultant and has completed research projects for, among others, the Institute of Economic Affairs (where he is a Fellow), the South African government and numerous private companies and organisations. Richard is director of economic policy at the health NGO, Africa Fighting Malaria. He has conducted a considerable amount of research into the political economy of malaria control and has published widely on the topic, including opinion pieces in *Business Day* in South Africa and the *Wall Street Journal Europe*.

FOREWORD

This is an excellent review of the devastation malaria has caused in the past and the economic problems a proposed worldwide ban on the use of DDT is causing for a developing African nation, Mozambique. It is about more than that, though. It is about the kinds of problems we create when we allow a single agenda to force policy development without thinking through the possible consequences.

One of the greatest achievements of the twentieth century was the eradication of smallpox. It took a long time, a lot of effort and a lot of resources to achieve that. There has not been a new case of smallpox in three decades and hopefully there never will be another. Euphoric with this achievement, nations agreed to destroy virtually all the known stocks of the wild virus. Only the USA and the Russians were allowed to keep any and that in very small amounts. But most experts believe that some rogue states or organisations have retained stocks and may be trying to create biological weapons from smallpox. Today the vast majority of the world's population is unprotected against smallpox. Meanwhile, the amounts of smallpox vaccine have dwindled almost to non-existence. Some scientists, medical experts and politicians are now questioning the wisdom of the decision to get rid of the smallpox stocks.

Today there are other efforts under way to develop international treaties, for example to reduce carbon dioxide emissions into the atmosphere. Carbon dioxide is a greenhouse gas that is increasing in the atmosphere and thought to be contributing to global warming. The effort to ban the use of DDT worldwide, the subject of this review, is another example. The highly developed nations of the world rid their populations of malaria decades ago. They achieved this by using DDT and other insecticides, draining wetlands, providing physical barriers like screens and nets to keep mosquitoes away from people and using anti-malarial agents. Now these same nations are telling the rest of the world, even nations like Mozambique, that they must join in a worldwide ban of DDT. The reason for this is that after decades of use it was apparent that DDT was persistent, and had bio-accumulated up food chains and in ecosystems. It weakened the eggs of some wild birds and their numbers declined dramatically. When this connection to DDT was recognised its use was decreased and even stopped in much of the world. The endangered bird species have now begun to recover. Scientists now know that DDT cannot be used ubiquitously against malaria. But it can be used safely if it is used sparingly and in combination with other techniques. Malaria is still endemic in many developing nations. It represents an enormous health and economic burden for them. Sick people cannot work, they cannot find food, and they cannot care for their children. These nations need all the tools available to get rid of this disease. Limiting them by banning the use of DDT, which is still the most effective agent available to combat malaria, may prove to be as unwise as some of the decisions made earlier about smallpox.

Another great achievement of the twentieth century was an incredible increase in personal material wealth and standards of living. Though the increase in wealth is extraordinary, its unequal distribution is even more extraordinary. The nations that were rich at the beginning of the twentieth century have seen their material wealth explode. Nations that were poor at the beginning of the twentieth century have grown richer too, but much more slowly. The relative gulf between rich and poor nations has grown and today is larger than at any time in history. Malaria is still endemic in most of the world's poor nations. Tren and Bate have done an admirable job of exposing the follies of a DDT ban.

A worldwide ban on DDT may not be a good idea, at least not yet. DDT should remain available for focused and controlled use to help nations where the disease remains. If DDT is banned then what we are really doing is moving back to a form of imperialism that will significantly hobble economic development in poor nations. Banning DDT will cause the gap between rich and poor nations to continue to expand.

HAROLD M. KOENIG, MD
Vice Admiral, US Navy (retired)
Former US Navy Surgeon General
President, The Annapolis Center
November 2000

SUMMARY

- Malaria imposes colossal costs on mankind, in terms of lives lost, ill health and impaired economic development. Over 1 million people, mostly children, die from the disease each year and over 300 million fall sick.
- Malaria is primarily a developing country disease, but it was not always so. Much of Europe and North America were malarial up to the early 1950s, but spraying the pesticide DDT eradicated the disease from these areas.
- Vector control (killing the anopheles mosquito) using DDT was pursued as a one-weapon policy after World War II in most malarial areas. While DDT was remarkably successful in many areas, it was not always appropriate.
- Despite a lack of scientific evidence, DDT was banned in many countries in the early 1970s following concerns about its environmental and human health impacts. However, the negative impacts from DDT use in agriculture, which led to the concerns, are vastly different from the impacts of DDT used in health control.
- The environmental impacts of DDT use in disease control are negligible and indeed its use could be beneficial to the environment. In addition, no scientific peer-reviewed study has ever replicated any case of negative human health impacts

from DDT. Nevertheless, environmental pressure groups and donor agencies disapprove of the use of DDT and actively campaign for its withdrawal.

- Although malaria is a developing country problem, much of the malaria control policy is formulated by developed country agencies. As a result, developing countries are frequently required to follow malaria control programmes that are not necessarily ideal or even applicable to local circumstances.
- Following a more politically correct and purportedly environmentally friendly policy, many health agencies, donor agencies and governments withdrew their support for DDT, and pesticide use in general, in disease control. The higher costs of the alternatives and the development of mosquito resistance to many alternatives increase the importance of DDT use.
- Many countries have been encouraged to control malaria with drug programmes and bed nets alone, repeating the mistakes of following one-track control programmes of the past.
- In December 2000, country delegates to the UNEP Persistent Organic Pollutants (POPs) Convention Negotiating Conference showed their support for the use of DDT in disease control, by granting exemption and allowing continued use of the chemical.
- Negative perceptions and pressure from wealthy developed countries still frustrate the use of DDT in disease control and add to the millions that die and suffer every year.

TABLES

Table 1a Amounts and costs of insecticides for indoor spraying during 1997/98 season for Mpumalanga, Northern Province and KwaZulu-Natal, South Africa   70

Table 1b Comparative costs per structure and per m² of different insecticides: 1997/98 spraying season for Mpumalanga, Northern Province and KwaZulu-Natal, South Africa   71

Table 2 Malaria cases – KwaZulu-Natal   72

Table 3 The cost of various insecticides used for adult mosquito control   73

Table 4 Summary of non-vector control economic costs of malaria: Mozal project   83

Table 5 Vector control and education costs for Mozal and SDI   85

Table 6 Loss of economic growth in 31 malaria-endemic African countries, 1980–95   88

Box 1 Administering a spraying programme   38

Box 2 The development of resistance   66

Chart 1 Comparison of representatives to POPs INC5 meeting   51

Malaria and the DDT Story

1 INTRODUCTION

Malaria has probably accounted for more deaths and has influenced the course of history more than any other disease. It has had a disastrous effect on economic development throughout the world and continues to do so in some of the world's poorest developing countries. While malaria today is associated with tropical countries, it is only within the last fifty years that malaria has been driven out of the temperate and developed countries of the North.[1]

Even before Ronald Ross proved in 1898 that the plasmodium parasite that causes malaria was passed to man by the female anopheles mosquito, efforts to control malaria were swayed and influenced by political and economic agendas. The main methods of control have been prevention (stopping the disease-carrying mosquito – vector – from contacting humans) and cure (treating the parasitical infection).

Shortly after World War II, malaria affected numerous countries, including the United States and Europe as far north as Holland, as well as the less developed, tropical South. Post-war malaria control strategies were to a very large extent determined by the Northern countries, and proved remarkably successful.

---

[1] The literature often refers to a 'war' or other 'military' metaphors against malaria. This is partly because the increase in post World War II malaria resulted from destruction of irrigation and water-control systems by retreating armies (see Harrison, 1978).

Even though malaria control strategies failed in some Southern countries and the disease is spreading and increasing in these countries at alarming rates, the malaria control agenda is still dictated by Northern countries.

At the beginning of the 21st century, Mozambique, one of the world's poorest countries, is battling to control malaria and to build a viable economy after seventeen years of destructive civil war. Mozambique's anti-malaria efforts are being hampered by Northern country policy. This policy, which may be appropriate for rich countries, is being promoted as a sensible approach for poor countries.

This paper examines historic malaria control policies and draws parallels between the political and economic forces behind those policies and the situation today. It then analyses the effect of the disease and different control efforts on economic development in Southern African nations. A special focus will be the role of the pesticide DDT and the current political campaign to ban its use. The paper uses the Mozal Aluminium Smelter in Mozambique and its malaria control activities as a case study. Mozal displays all the current problems of and solutions to malaria control: the poverty of less developed countries which find it hard to address malaria adequately; the desire of wealthy western industrial investors to rid their workforce of malaria; the lack of new technologies to combat third world diseases, such as malaria; and the dominance of political correctness in international aid agencies, which do more harm than good by denying less developed countries the right to use DDT.

Finally the paper discusses possible future malaria control strategies, based on the lessons learned from the Mozal case study and from other sources.

2 HISTORICAL MALARIA CONTROL POLICIES

Malaria control policies have been in place in many countries for hundreds of years. Most policies were based on land drainage and the removal of standing water. Although the link between the *plasmodium* parasite, the anopheles mosquito and man was only made in 1898, malaria has long been associated with swamps, marshes and wetlands. Without the knowledge that these were breeding grounds for mosquitoes, people thought that foul smelling air[1] or miasmas[2] were the cause of infection. Others believed that poisons seeped from the soil into drinking water, thereby infecting people (Harrison, 1978: 26).

The ancient method of planting swamps with water-loving and aromatic eucalyptus trees rapidly dried out wetlands and so reduced malaria rates. The miasma theory gave rise to the view held by monks in the Roman Campagnia that the aromatic property of the trees acted as a shield against the malaria poisons and was also an antidote (Harrison, 1978: 26). This practice continued in modern Italy, where malaria was endemic until the mid-twentieth century (Croumbie Brown, 1890). Confusion was also widespread among the early European settlers in Southern Africa. As the settlers frequently camped near water, rates of malaria were high and

---

1   The word malaria comes from Italian, *mal* – bad, *aria* – air.

2   Miasmas are defined as infectious or noxious exhalations from putrescent organic matter (*Shorter Oxford English Dictionary*).

this frequently frustrated their efforts to settle and develop the land. It was widely believed that malaria was caused not by disease-carrying mosquitoes, but was somehow caused by the *Acacia xanthophloea* tree – commonly known as the fever tree[3] (van Wyk, 1984).

In 1889, France's efforts to construct the Panama Canal were abandoned due to financial scandals, which brought disgrace on national political figures. The ten-year project caused the loss of millions of dollars and thousands of lives to malaria and yellow fever (Baird, 1999). Working on the miasma theory – of the infection seeping up from the ground – the beds of malaria patients were raised off the ground and the feet stood in cups of water. US efforts to complete the canal, ten years later, benefited from an understanding of vector control, which followed from acceptance of Ross's crucial discovery.

Environmental vector control

The understanding that the malaria parasite was transferred to man by the anopheles mosquito helped to focus habitat removal efforts and allowed them to be more effective.

The fight against malaria in Italy was championed by, among others, social reformers such as Angelo Celli who argued that malaria control should be achieved by ensuring that the poor agricultural workers (who were most at risk) were better fed, better housed and had increased wages. Part of Celli's strategy was to reclaim swamps and resettle people on this land (Bruce-Chwatt &

---

3   The *Acacia xanthophloea* has a yellow trunk – a colour often linked with disease, which helped to entrench the belief that the tree was somehow associated with malaria.

Zulueta, 1980: 94). Apart from the specific malaria control programmes, increasing populations, technological advancement and a rise in demand for agricultural land led to drainage of many swamps in Europe and a subsequent reduction in malaria rates.

After Ronald Ross, a military doctor working in India, had discovered the cause of malaria, he was charged with controlling mosquitoes in the British Empire. Sierra Leone was Britain's first West African colony. Endemic malaria and yellow fever made the whole area unhealthy, which hampered efforts to develop commerce and trade. Freetown, Sierra Leone's capital, had a particularly bad sewage and rainwater drainage system. Puddles suitable for mosquito breeding were to be found everywhere. Ross first mapped and then applied petroleum to all the breeding sites to kill larvae. However, the task was bigger than Ross and his relatively small team had anticipated. It eventually became impossible continually to clear all breeding sites and in 1902 a decision was made to move all European settlers to a segregated settlement above Freetown that had fewer mosquitoes and a reduced risk of disease (Harrison, 1978: 121–9).

Malaria control efforts were also made in Lagos, Nigeria at the turn of the century where the governor, Sir William MacGregor, who had a medical background, was determined to make the city safe for both Europeans and the indigenous population. His approach was far broader than Ross's as he arranged for public lectures to educate the population on the disease, arranged for the malarial cure, quinine (made from the bark of the cinchona tree) to be made widely available free of charge and set about draining the swamps in the midst of which Lagos was built. Despite his efforts, the war on malaria in Lagos was lost, as Sir William's efforts were simply not enough. Even his broad range of anti-malaria 'tools' was not sufficient to keep the mosquito at bay. Clearly, he did not have the technology or pesticides to ensure that all breeding sites were eradicated. Furthermore, the population was insufficiently educated about malaria transmission, even though he spent as much as £10,000 per year, worth more than £4 million in today's money (Harrison, 1978: 131).

According to a publication that MacGregor wrote in 1901 in the *British Medical Journal* (1901, II: 680–2), called 'Notes on anti-malarial measures now being taken in Lagos', it was 'painfully apparent that what is being done at Lagos against malaria is far short of what is required' (Harrison, 1978: 131). His approach was not to segregate the Europeans and the indigenous population. He felt that the success of the empire rested on a healthy native population. These ideas were far too progressive at the time. Dr Stevens from the Royal Society's Malaria Commission described MacGregor's efforts to protect the native population as 'dangerous sentimentality'. Therefore, after Sir William died of the disease in 1903, the programme was abandoned (Harrison, 1978: 130–1).

A British military base known as Mian Mir in the Punjab province of India had extremely high incidences of malaria after irrigation canals were constructed in 1851.[4] The irrigation canals provided ideal breeding habitats for mosquitoes and, due to the severity of malaria at the beginning of the twentieth century, it was decided to clear and oil the irrigation ditches, remove infected people and administer quinine in order to both prevent and cure the disease.

---

4   The annual incidence of malaria was often 100%, meaning the entire population was infected with the parasite. During epidemics this would rise to over 300%, meaning individuals would suffer from at least three bouts of malaria in a year (Harrison, 1978: 131).

The malaria control efforts at Mian Mir proved to be extremely expensive but had remarkably little effect on the incidence of malaria and the numbers of mosquitoes. The control effort at Mian Mir was '. . . so exceptionally expensive, not just in money, but in the use of involuntary labour that even if it had succeeded, it could rarely, if ever, have been emulated' (Harrison, 1978: 134).

The problem in Mian Mir was that they had not counted on the fact that mosquitoes could travel. They thought that mosquitoes could not go very far, but they found that the adults simply flew in from other areas and the larvae also migrated in by water. So as fast as they oiled the irrigation ditches and cleaned out pools, the mosquito population just replenished itself from outside.[5]

Vector control programmes were more successful in other areas, such as in Klang in Malaysia where the removal of jungles and marshes from in and around the town led to a dramatic reduction in malaria cases. In 1903, after the jungle and marshes had been cleared, hospital admissions for 'fever' were one-tenth of the normal level (Harrison, 1978: 137). The success at Klang was most likely because the *Anopheles umbrosis*, the chief vector, would not lay eggs in full sunlight and therefore retreated when the jungle was cleared.

Chemical vector control

The development of the larvicide Paris Green made an important contribution to vector control as it proved effective and cheap and

---

5 Similarly, *Anopheles funestus* has reappeared in South Africa by flying in from Mozambique – the same problem occurring a hundred years later (Coetzee, 2000).

was relatively easy to apply. Other larviciding efforts included introducing larvivorous fish (*Gambusia affinis*) and, as mentioned above, the application of petroleum to breeding sites. In South Africa, Paris Green was used relatively effectively during the 1930s. Some larviciding programmes were remarkably successful in South Africa. The South African Railways for example managed to reduce the number of malaria cases among its staff from 1,021 to 57 between 1932 and 1938, chiefly through sustained larviciding programmes (SA Department of Health, 1997: 5).

Pyrethrum insecticide[6] was introduced to the Panama Canal malaria control programme in 1901, where it was burned like incense inside sealed houses (Harrison, 1978: 161). On its own, pyrethrum used in this way did not reduce malaria incidence, as it was only used in houses where a fever was reported. While the burning of the pyrethrum may have been effective in killing mosquitoes, there were plenty of asymptomatic carriers that were not targeted.[7] Therefore a far wider programme was required.

A spray version of the insecticide was invented in 1913 but was not used for malaria control until South Africa adopted pyrethrum spraying in 1930, when it became the main method of vector control and was used with great success (Harrison, 1978: 210; Sharp et al., 1998). Not only were the pyrethrum sprays more effective in killing the malaria vector, but they cost around one third of the larval control programme (Sharp et al., 1988). A problem with the pyrethrum spraying was that it had to be repeated

6 Pyrethrum is a natural insecticide derived from a species of chrysanthemum (Harrison, 1978: 161).

7 Pyrethrum burners were only placed in houses where people showed symptoms of malaria because of cost. However, it is possible to carry malaria without showing symptoms.

weekly during the main transmission season and its use was therefore labour intensive.

The next major advance in vector control came in the form of DDT. Like pyrethrum sprays, DDT had been synthesised and used in agriculture before it was introduced as an anti-malaria tool. DDT was developed in the 1930s to control insect pests in farming (and was used to this effect in Switzerland), but was first used in substantial quantities by the military in World War II to control body lice which carried typhus. Its subsequent introduction to the fight against malaria had dramatic effects the world over. However, as described below, not every country was to witness long-term victory against the disease.

3 DRUG THERAPY AGAINST MALARIA

Historic drug policies

The bark of the cinchona tree has been used to make quinine for hundreds of years. It was Jesuit missionaries in South America who discovered the anti-malarial properties of quinine and the drug was first exported to Europe in the 1630s and later to India in 1657. The Jesuits promoted the use of the 'Cardinal's Bark' throughout the world, but its acceptance in Europe was not universal. Orthodox physicians were sceptical of the drug and refused to prescribe it, although this reluctance was partly because the drug was frequently of poor quality and 'adulterated with inert bitter substances' (Bruce-Chwatt & Zulueta, 1980: 92). Others' reluctance was based on faith rather than reason: some Protestants refused to take the drug, preferring to die rather than be saved by Jesuits' powder (Bruce-Chwatt & Zulueta, 1980: 133).

Quinine became one of the main strategies to fight malaria as both a treatment and a prophylactic. Quinine became popular in Italy towards the end of the nineteenth century when the anti-malaria campaign was headed by social reformers like Celli. Robert Koch, the German pioneer of bacteriology, was so impressed with quinine that he declared in 1899 that 'quinine systematically administered to both new and relapsed cases would wipe out malaria in nine months' (Harrison, 1978: 172). What

Koch failed to appreciate was that people could carry the plasmodium parasite and not necessarily feel ill. Screening every person's blood to determine whether or not he or she carried the parasite was not feasible as the tests were time consuming and not entirely accurate. Koch's approach was never likely to eliminate the disease.

Italy passed a number of acts to help control malaria, many of which were designed to promote social change as well. For example, legislation extended the availability of quinine, and increased the responsibility of landowners to protect workers, control mosquitoes and report malaria cases. The laws achieved little in the way of social change, but quinine sales rose dramatically after a law was passed on 23 December 1900, which set up a state quinine service.

Celli, the social reformer, had lobbied strongly for quinine-based malaria control legislation, despite being a critic of Koch's approach. The 1900 Act ensured that all quinine was sold by the state with profits being used for quinine distribution to the poor and for research and special prizes (Harrison, 1978: 174). Celli was a founder member of the Societa per gli Studi della Malaria that aimed to promote research and lobby for health legislation. It is likely therefore that Celli and his organisation would have profited from the research grants accruing from the sale of quinine.

Italian state sales of quinine rose from 2,242 kg in 1902/3 to 24,000 kg in 1914. During this time, malaria incidence fell significantly and mortality decreased from 15,000 to just over 2,000 (Bruce-Chwatt & Zulueta, 1980: 94). While the distribution of quinine will have played an important part in ensuring that the malaria rates were so successfully reduced, quinine's role has been exaggerated. Malaria had in fact been declining in Italy for many decades with changes in climate, expansions of agricultural land and general economic development (Harrison, 1978: 174).

Quinine was widely used in other parts of Europe without the kind of legislation that was passed in Italy. In the United Kingdom, where the effects of malaria had been known about for many centuries, the Protestants overcame their initial objection to the Jesuits' powder and accepted quinine. The use of quinine along with the reclamation of swamps and marshes and a general improvement in medical care saw malaria rates decline in England from the 1850s onwards (Bruce-Chwatt & Zulueta, 1980: 137).

Current drug policies

Quinine still plays an important part in the treatment of malaria and in many countries is the drug of choice for complicated or severe malaria. Quinine has strong unpleasant side effects and it is therefore often administered intravenously to hospitalised patients. Up to 70% of patients who take quinine, for example, can experience tinnitus, vertigo and nausea that lasts throughout the dosage period (SA Department of Health, 1996). It is not surprising that there is low compliance when patients are required to take quinine tablets without supervision. After World War II, chloroquine was the preferred prophylactic and treatment for malaria. However resistance began to emerge in the early 1960s in Southeast Asia and South America and has subsequently spread to most other malarial countries, with the exception of Central America, the Caribbean and the Middle East (Baird, 1999).

Chloroquine resistance has dealt a very severe blow to the fight against malaria. Some researchers point to drug resistance as the single most important factor contributing to the rise in the worldwide incidence of malaria. Chloroquine is not only a cheap drug, but it is relatively easy to administer and does not have the serious side effects of quinine.

In countries where there is chloroquine resistance, administration of the drug can even promote the transmission of the disease. This is because the use of chloroquine culls any chloroquine-sensitive parasites and leaves resistant trophozoites to differentiate to gametocytes. What this means is that the most robust parasites will be left to thrive in a less competitive environment (Baird, 1999: 23). Chloroquine-treated patients will feel better quickly, but they will maintain asymptomatic levels of the parasite and remain infectious to the anopheline mosquitoes. This ensures that a mobile pool of asymptomatic carriers of the drug-resistant strain remains and can infect new mosquitoes.[1]

In Southern Africa, the main drug used in the treatment of uncomplicated malaria is sulfadoxine-pyrimethamine (SP), which is taken orally and has proved effective. In KwaZulu-Natal province of South Africa, resistance to SP has developed in recent years and is supplemented with chloroquine. KwaZulu-Natal province has the highest malaria rates in South Africa and is also the main transit route for migrating people from Mozambique to South Africa. It is thought that asymptomatic carriers of the malaria parasite from Mozambique introduced SP resistant strains of the parasite to the province (Maharaj, 2000). The resistance rates to SP in KwaZulu-Natal are approximately 56%, while in the other two

---

1   The mobility of asymptomatic carriers is important, as carriers will introduce new strains of the parasite to new areas. The relaxation of border controls in South Africa since 1994 and the subsequent movement of people within Southern Africa is very likely to have contributed to the rise in malaria rates in the region.

malarial provinces of South Africa, Mpumalanga and Northern Province, the resistance rates are less than 10% and zero, respectively. The WHO recommends that a drug should no longer be used when resistance exceeds 20% (Maharaj, 2000). There is far less migration from Mozambique through these other provinces, which adds weight to the theory that resistance has been imported from Mozambique.

Using combination drug therapies is widely accepted as a reliable strategy to counter the problem of drug resistance, especially as there is little prospect of development of new effective drugs. Using combination therapies ensures that the life span of both drugs is extended and it thereby reduces the likelihood that asymptomatic carriers of the malaria parasite will spread the disease. South Africa is currently attempting to introduce co-arthemeter, another combination therapy, to KwaZulu-Natal (Maharaj, 2000).

As malaria occurs predominantly in less developed countries with low purchasing power, the potential market for new antimalarial drugs is relatively small. Without a viable market, pharmaceutical companies have been reluctant to invest in the development of new drugs because they could not justify the considerable expenditure in research and development and administrative approval, with little prospect of a return on their investment.

According to Desowitz (1993), 'the best anti-malarial hope on today's horizon is a "new" two thousand-year-old drug called Qinghaosu.' Decocted from the leaves of sweet wormwood, the recipe was found in a book written in AD 340, and rediscovered after a search through the ancient Chinese herbal pharmacopoeia begun in 1967. The drug has been shown to be effective against cerebral malaria and against strains solidly resistant to chloro-quine. It has been chemically analysed and could be mass-pro-duced, but so far the opportunity has not been taken up.[2]

In a recent development, scientists at Cambridge University (NAS, 2000) have found that a drug called clotrimazole, which has long been used to treat fungal infections in humans, also has a strong anti-malarial effect. Test-tube trials showed that the drug kills a strain of the parasite *plasmodium falciparum* that causes a particularly severe form of malaria in humans. The concentrations of the drug used to kill the parasite were similar to those known to be attained in human blood after taking the drug orally. Because clotrimazole is already known to be clinically safe, and free of re-sistance reactions by fungi, it holds some promise as an effective way to combat the disease.

Researchers are currently seeking funding to initiate a pilot clinical trial of clotrimazole in Iquitos, Peru, where malaria caused by drug-resistant parasites has become a major public health con-cern.

Vaccine

The history of the search for a malaria vaccine is replete with unre-alistic optimism, data manipulation and even fraud (Desowitz, 1992). The development of a malaria vaccine has been widely re-ported. However an effective vaccine is not likely to be made avail-able for at least another seven years (De Gregori, 1998), although it has been 'just around the corner' for several decades. Even when a

---

2   Mefloquine is still efficacious, but being a synthetic analogue of quinine, some users suffer similar side effects.

malaria vaccine is produced, it is unlikely that the poorest nations will be able to buy enough to protect all those at risk. This situation has led to calls for a Vaccine Purchase Fund by the Harvard Centre for International Development (CID) that would provide a guaranteed market for vaccines once they were developed.[3]

While drug therapy has to be part of any malaria control programme, sole reliance or over-emphasis on this form of control is extremely dangerous for the reasons described above. Despite these dangers, however, drug therapy and the use of 'smart' technology form a major part of the World Health Organization's (WHO) Roll Back Malaria programme (RBM).

In the past, malaria control strategies were more often than not determined politically, with scant regard for the practical requirements of malarial regions or indeed the best prevailing method of control at the time. This trend continues, but today politics appear to be driven by environmentalist groups in developed countries. Then as now, the casualties in this political war are the victims of malaria in the world's poorest countries.

---

3   For more on the Vaccine Purchase Fund see www.cid.harvard.edu/cidmalaria/ malaria.htm

4 DDT AND THE GLOBAL ERADICATION CAMPAIGN

We have discovered many preventatives against tropical diseases and often against insects of all kinds, from lice to mosquitoes . . . The excellent DDT powder, which has been fully experimented with and found to yield astonishing results, will henceforth be used on a great scale by the British forces in Burma, and the American and Australian forces in the Pacific and India and in all theatres.

Winston Churchill, 28 September 1944
(quoted in Mellanby, 1992: 23)

The concept that the world could be completely cleared of the disease was born with the successful eradication of *Aedes aegypti* and later *Anopheles gambiae*[1] from Brazil. The eradication in Brazil was primarily due to the work and financial support of the Rockefeller Foundation[2] under the guidance of Fred Soper who initiated a wide-ranging larviciding and vector control programme using oil, Paris Green and pyrethrum sprays. Soper's goal was to eradicate the malaria vector from Brazil. *Anopheles aegypti* was eradicated in 1934, and by the mid 1940s *Anopheles gambiae* was similarly wiped out.

---

1   *Anopheles gambiae*, a highly efficient vector, is suspected of having travelled aboard ship from Africa to Brazil.

2   The Rockefeller Foundation was founded by the oil tycoon John D. Rockefeller in 1901, with the aim of promoting the well-being of mankind.

DDT and chloroquine were introduced for malaria control by the US military by 1944 and after the end of World War II they were in wide use around the world. The use of the pesticide led to enormous optimism and the belief that malaria could be eradicated from the entire globe. The reasons for this optimism were not hard to see. DDT was, and is, highly effective in killing the malaria vector and interrupting the transfer of the malaria parasite. It is also cheap, safe and easy to use which put it within reach of even the poorest countries' health budgets. Shortly after the end of World War II there was also a conviction that vector control, and in particular pesticide spraying, was the only way in which the disease could be tackled.

The early successes of DDT were nothing short of spectacular. Scientists 'thought that the whole literature of agricultural and medical entomology would have to be re-written ... because of the use of DDT' (Mellanby, 1992: 37). In Europe and North America, DDT was widely used and, within a few years, malaria had been eradicated from both continents. It is thought that in one year alone, the transmission of malaria in Greece came to a halt (Harrison, 1978). Mack-Smith even suggested that malaria eradication 'was the most important single fact in the whole of modern Italian history' (1959: 494).

In South Africa, the malaria control programme adopted DDT in 1946 and, shortly afterwards, the number of cases in the Transvaal declined to about one tenth of the number of cases reported in 1942/3. In some areas of South Africa, DDT spraying was so successful that it was stopped altogether and only reintroduced after periods of heavy rains, when malaria cases tended to rise.

Perhaps the most remarkable success story was to be found in Sri Lanka (then Ceylon). DDT spraying began in 1946 and, as with

South Africa, was an instant success with the island's death rate from malaria falling from 20.3 to 14.3 per thousand. Within ten years, DDT use had cut the incidence of malaria down from around three million cases to 7,300 and had eliminated all malaria deaths (Harrison, 1978). By 1964, the number of malaria cases had been reduced to just 29 and at the time it was assumed that the war against malaria in Sri Lanka had been won.

After World War II, India also had a particularly bad malaria problem, where every year around 75 million people contracted the disease and about 800,000 died. Almost the entire country was malarial; then, as now, there were six anopheline mosquito vectors. By using DDT, India managed to bring the number of cases down from the estimated 75 million in 1951 to around 50,000 in 1961 (Harrison, 1978: 247). The achievement of reducing the number of infections to this degree cannot be overstated, but the success in India, as in many other countries, was to be short lived.

Eradication of malaria was achieved in only ten countries, four of which were in Europe, and the other six in the Americas and the Caribbean. The WHO strategy of eliminating malaria from the globe did not stretch over much of Africa, where the vast majority of cases occurred and indeed still occur. It had been hoped that the swift and decisive use of DDT through well planned and funded malaria control programmes throughout the world would achieve success. For poorer countries without sufficient health care resources or transport infrastructure the plans were not appropriate and goals were gradually scaled back from eradication to control to containment.

The Global Malaria Eradication Campaign, adopted by the World Health Assembly in May 1955, relied on vector control as the main method of interruption of transmission of the disease,

> **Box 1 Administering a spraying programme**
> Successful spraying programmes need to be well organised with detailed maps of the malarial areas and a systematic plan to the spraying programme. Sprayers need to target the areas most at risk and it is vital that all structures within an area are sprayed, as omitting some will undermine the programme. In addition, spraying needs to be followed up with an epidemiological study to measure the efficacy of the pesticides and also to administer blood tests for parasite levels within the communities. All this requires a significant amount of funding, organisation and commitment from the sprayers, medical staff and higher bureaucratic structures. Malaria control programmes must take account of the capacity 'on the ground' to implement them and where capacity is lacking, the programme should provide resources and expertise. This 'capacity gap' is an important factor in the ultimate failure of the many mosquito eradication plans.

and was later to be followed up by case detection and treatment. Mathematical models developed by Professor George MacDonald showed that eradication was possible if the proposed vector control programme was followed. The United States Agency for International Development (USAID) played a major role in supporting and financing the initiative and contributed $1.2 billion to the programme between 1950 and 1972. The WHO contributed far less, with $20.3 million between 1956 and 1963, of which $17.5 million was from the United States. All other countries combined contributed only $2.8 million (Baird, 1999: 14).

One of the reasons that the WHO pushed for rapid implementation of DDT spraying for an intensive and limited time period was because of fears of resistance to the pesticide. The problems of resistance[3] to DDT first emerged in Greece in the early 1950s where it was observed that the main Greek vector, *Anopheles sacharovi*, showed physiological resistance to the pesticide. Resistance to DDT was later observed in the Middle East, parts of Indonesia and also in northern Nigeria in 1956.

Fears about the increase in resistance to DDT (and dieldrin, another organochlorine pesticide) led the WHO expert committee in 1956 to call for the swift and overwhelming vector control programmes that would eliminate the pool of parasites before resistance could develop. Many countries did not have the infrastructure or organisational capacity to implement the WHO plans. India's initial successes, for example, were reversed largely because it could not sustain the vector control programme. Malaria control officers were not properly trained and were frequently careless in their approach to spraying and detecting malaria cases (Harrison, 1978: 250).

Before long, malaria rates began to rise in many of the countries that had all but eradicated the disease. The resurgence was partly caused by complacency following the early successes. Some countries decided to cut back on their programmes in order to save money and others simply became careless. Many developing countries could not have anticipated that the vector control 'blitzkrieg' would have to be sustained over a longer period than originally planned by the WHO.

The unilateral vector eradication approach to malaria control that constituted the Global Eradication Campaign could have led to its ultimate failure. Whether eradicating the disease is or is not

---

3   See Box 2, p.66 for a fuller discussion of resistance to pesticides.

technically feasible, the approach followed by the USAID under the guise of the WHO imposed unrealistic control strategies that could not be sustained in most poor countries. DDT was remarkably successful in almost all the countries in which it was used, but it was never likely to work as a magic bullet. Malaria is a disease that is influenced by several factors, such as climate and migration, as well as the control strategies. Developing a malaria control strategy that is solely reliant on vector control – especially on only one pesticide – was optimistic at best and foolish at worst. The greater folly was in the unilateral way in which the policy was developed, which failed to take into account the conditions under which the policy would be implemented.

As will be described below, however, far from learning from these errors, the WHO and donor agencies, such as USAID, continue to promote policies unilaterally. The basis for recommending malaria control weapons has changed, but the political reality – in which the agenda for malaria control strategies is determined by developed countries and imposed on developing countries – remains.

There were critics of the eradication campaign from the beginning. The most cogent arguments centred on the over-reliance on DDT, but there were other complaints. It was alleged that vector control was promoted to encourage capitalist development and to fight communism, furthering American political aims, rather than always doing what was best for local people (see next section for alternative methods of malaria control). For example, 'The real (or imagined) fear that the [Italian] government[4] would be won over

---

4   Speaking at the Third Session of a joint WHO/FAO meeting on malaria in 1948, Missiroli of Italy noted that the prosperity of Europe depended on the possibility of exploiting Africa. 'Africa cannot be fully exploited because of the danger of flies

by the communists at the next election was used to justify continued external funding for malaria control, even though this was no longer technically required' (Litsios, 1997: 270).

Furthermore, Litsios (1997: 272) claims that WHO was in a difficult position from inception, 'caught in the middle of the problem created by the emergency needs following World War II and the political intricacies of the Cold War'. The USSR left WHO in 1949 and did not return until 1957, and hence no malaria specialists from the Southern, malarial, regions of the USSR were included in malaria control efforts.

Certain commentators espoused the neo-Malthusian line that it may be unkind to keep people from 'dying from malaria so that they could die more slowly of starvation', and even saw malaria as 'a blessing in disguise, since a large proportion of the malaria belt is not suited to agriculture, and the disease has helped to keep man from destroying it – and from wasting his substance upon it' (Vogt, 1949: 13, 28). The modern-day green version of this is stated by Gell-Man: 'Some day anti-malarial vaccines will probably be developed, which may even wipe out the various forms of the disease entirely, but then another difficulty will arise: important wild areas that had been protected by the dangers of malaria will be exposed to unwise development' (1994: 353).

Plus ça change – past and present malaria control policies

Ross's discovery that the anopheles mosquito transmitted the

---

and mosquitoes; if we can control them, the prosperity of Europe will be enhanced', cited in Litsios (1997: 281).

malaria parasite was a crucial step in attempts to control the disease. But the discovery was not universally embraced and some involved in malaria control rejected its potential value – namely supporters of the 'Italian way'. In choosing political doctrine over sound scientific and medical research, the so-called social reformers ignored a vital malaria control weapon. On the other hand, those who were single-minded in their pursuit of vector control as the only way in which to combat the disease, such as the Rockefeller Institute, missed out on the potential of drug therapies.

Prior to the introduction of DDT into malaria control programmes, these two divergent approaches dominated efforts to control the disease. On the one hand, malaria was seen as much as a social problem as a medical and entomological one, by Celli and Koch and more recently by Litsios (1997) and Packard (1997).[5] This so-called Italian way of tackling the disease saw social reform, poverty reduction and the advancement of vulnerable communities as the main tools. The Italian way strongly favoured the use of quinine as the main practical way of eliminating the malaria parasite and, as described above, did this by passing legislation. The supporters of the Italian way were not confined to Italy. The influential Dutchman Professor Swellengrebel was also of the opinion that the fight against malaria should have two prongs, namely the reduction in mortality and improvement of social and economic conditions.[6] The Italian

---

5   Recent critics seem perturbed by the lack of consultation with local 'knowledge', and lack of general re-distribution of wealth, rather than promoting a particular vision.

6   Swellengrebel was not wedded to the idea of social and economic reform. During an investigation of malaria in the Union of South Africa in 1930, he

way favoured a centralised approach, and as described above, promoted the state control and supply of quinine.

The League of Nations Malaria Commission was set up in 1924 as an investigative unit and was active until 1937. Interestingly, according to Harrison, 'its mandate was cautiously restricted to stay well clear of any implications of international interference in national affairs' (Harrison, 1978: 183). The commission argued strongly in favour of quinine use, stating that over thirty years of vector control since Ross's discovery had produced 'a record of exaggerated expectations followed sooner or later by disappointment and abandonment of the work' (cited in Packard and Gadelha, 1997: 217).

On the other hand, the method of control favoured by the Rockefeller Foundation – the 'American way'– was founded in vector control and in particular the use of spray pesticides. Ronald Ross could be seen as one of the early founders of this approach, not only with his discovery of the role that the anopheles mosquito plays in the transmission of malaria, but also through his efforts to control malaria in Sierra Leone. The vector control successes of the Panama Canal and Brazil gave strength to the American way. Dr Lewis Hackett, who was sent by the Rockefeller Foundation to Italy to investigate malaria control, felt strongly that malaria could be defeated by attacking the mosquito. Importantly, he opposed the centralised control of the Italian way and was of the opinion one had to understand local conditions that allowed the disease to spread.

---

recommended 'species sanitation' as a main principle of control. He also recommended that no malaria control be conducted in certain parts of KwaZulu-Natal for fear of diminishing the natural immunity of the population.

But the commission only visited Europe and seemed to ignore the rest of the malarial world. It ignored much of the work by Ross and Hackett and maintained that the only effective way to fight malaria was through quinine. The League's proposals were widely criticised by those who saw merit in attacking the malaria vector.

Although the League's commission later softened its criticism of the Rockefeller Foundation and the American way, the two approaches never found common ground. While the commission continued to support drug therapy as the main method of control, in its last report it noted that the elimination of malaria by drug therapy and prophylaxis 'has not hitherto been found possible in practice' (cited in Harrison, 1978: 186).

The Rockefeller Foundation continued with its vector control approach, which in time came to dominate all malaria control work. Vector control was further entrenched as the main method of malaria control once DDT was introduced and had such spectacular successes in so many countries.

Ironically the Soper/Rockefeller Foundation approach – centralised spray management based on DDT, ignoring both medical treatment and often local social issues – was to establish a model which although effectual could not continue to live up to its billing of mosquito eradication. Neither was it any more sensitive than the Malaria Commission to local culture and requirements. Once it was partially discredited it too was soon abandoned (see Brown, 1997). The goal was gradually scaled back from mosquito eradication to malaria eradication and then malaria control in East Asia and Southern Africa and merely containment in Sub-Saharan Africa.

5 ENVIRONMENTALISM AND MALARIA CONTROL

While DDT was used in malaria control campaigns and also in agriculture, concerns were raised about the environmental impacts of the pesticide.[1] Perhaps the best-known attack on DDT was Rachel Carson's *Silent Spring*, published in 1962.[2] The book popularised the scare associated with DDT and claimed that it would have devastating impacts on birdlife, particularly birds higher up the food chain. The fears were based on the fact that DDT and its metabolites DDE and DDD accumulate in the body fat of animals. Even though many of the fears surrounding DDT were unfounded, and the studies upon which they were based unscientific, DDT was banned by the US Environmental Protection Agency in 1972.

Numerous scientific reports and evidence given by expert witnesses argued against a ban on DDT and in favour of its continued

1   Before World War II it was generally argued that malaria control could only be afforded if it contributed to agricultural development. For two decades from 1945 this link was dissolved (Litsios, 1997). But in recent decades a new parallel has emerged with the pre-war phase, in that although much medical control of malaria is done for humanitarian reasons, the only insecticides used in vector control are those that were developed for agriculture.

2   Entomologists and other scientists in Britain were aware of the potential environmental dangers of DDT in 1945. But at the time the acute toxicity problems from other pesticides, including organophosphate pesticides, dominated concerns of various governmental scientific committees (Mellanby, 1992: 83). There is also ample evidence to suggest that the potential impacts of DDT are reversible given sufficient time (Goklany, 2000d).

use. Despite this convincing evidence to the contrary, the EPA administrator, William Ruckelshaus, argued that the pesticide was '. . . a warning that man may be exposing himself to a substance that may ultimately have a serious effect on his health' (cited in Malkin & Fumento, 1999: 144). The pesticide was banned in the US in 1972 and in most other countries shortly after. However, it remained available for its crucial role as a medical pesticide. Ruckelshaus's preoccupations with potentially negative environmental and health impacts (despite all the evidence to the contrary), and his refusal to accept the scientific advice offered, most certainly contributed to death in malarial countries by denying them access to this life-saving pesticide.

The possibility that population control was an intentional aim of EPA policy has been raised by ex-EPA staff (Padden, 2000), but there is no explicit documentary evidence to support such a hypothesis.

Most developed countries followed the US lead and imposed bans on the chemical for all uses. Some developing countries also imposed a ban on the pesticide for agricultural use and some for all uses. For example, South Africa banned it for agricultural use in 1974. Sri Lankan officials had stopped using DDT in 1964, believing the malaria problem was solved, but by 1969 the number of malaria cases had risen from the low of 17 (achieved when DDT was used) to over 500,000 (Silva, 1997).

It is alleged that DDT was not widely re-introduced because of mosquito resistance to it, and DDT use was finally abandoned in favour of Malathion[3] in 1977 (Spielman, 1980). But a series of delete-

---

3   The introduction of alternative pesticides had disastrous results for those doing the spraying, with many deaths caused by poisoning from replacements. DDT is not harmful to humans. The DDT expert Kenneth Mellanby used to eat a pinch of DDT at every lecture he gave on DDT over a period of 40 years (Mellanby, 1992: 75).

rious positive feedbacks was established. 'It is likely that the reduction in support of spraying activities leading to inconsistent application of pesticides also played a role in the development of vector resistance' (Packard, 1997: 287). Furthermore, pressure not to use DDT may have been applied by western donors using resistance as a convenient argument. Recent evidence shows that even where resistance to DDT has emerged, the 'excito-repellancy' of DDT causes mosquitoes not to enter buildings that have been sprayed (Roberts et al., 2000). Under test conditions (see Grieco et al., 2000), for at least one type of malarial mosquito in Belize (the only country in which these tests have so far been conducted), DDT is far more successful than the most favoured vector control pesticide – Deltamethrin.[4] Hence it is unlikely that malaria rates would have increased (significantly) even if resistance were found. Recognising its continuing efficacy, many countries, such as those in Southern Africa, continue to allow DDT to be used for malaria control.

The concern about DDT came at a time when the environmentalist movement was beginning to gain both power and influence and the issue certainly added momentum to the movement. One of the key concepts of the movement is sustainable development, which achieved prominence largely through the efforts of Norwegian Prime Minister, Gro Harlem Brundtland, and the World Commission on Environment and Development's report in 1987, 'Our Common Future'. The commission said that:

Sustainable development is development that meets the needs of the present without compromising the ability of

---

4   Some malarial mosquitoes are resistant to Deltamethrin in Southern Africa, so the effectiveness of it will be even lower than in Belize.

future generations to meet their own needs. It contains
within it two key concepts:
the concept of 'needs', in particular the essential needs of
the world's poor, to which overriding priority should be
given; and
the idea of limitations imposed by the state of technology
and social organisation on the environment's ability to meet
present and future needs.

Commonwealth Secretariat, 2000

One interpretation of sustainable development, known as
strong sustainability, assumes that natural capital, such as forests,
wildlife and other natural resources, cannot be substituted for
other forms of capital, such as man-made capital. The use of pesticides would not be consistent within a strong sustainable development framework because of the negative effects it might have on
the natural capital.

Within malaria control, policies that try to fulfil the requirements of strong sustainability would not use pesticides or other
chemicals but would rather promote the use of bed nets or drug
therapies. The WHO and other leading world agencies have all
committed themselves to policies that are purported to be more in
line with this view of sustainable development and avoid the use of
potentially environmentally harmful chemicals. The WHO's
Global Malaria Control Strategy focuses on the improved clinical
management of malaria diagnosis and treatment rather than on
parasite control programmes.

The Roll Back Malaria programme, which is jointly sponsored
by the WHO and the World Bank, also focuses on the control of
malaria through diagnosis and treatment of malaria patients and
does not promote vector control. That the change of focus has

taken a markedly more 'environmental' stance should not be surprising given that the head of the WHO since 1997 has been Gro Harlem Brundtland (for details see www.who.int).

Donor agencies, malaria control and environmentalism

In 1995 the United Nations Environment Programme (UNEP) Governing Council (Decision 18/32, 25 May) decided to proceed with an instrument to control certain chemicals considered to 'pose major and increasing threats to human health and the environment' (http://irtpc.unep.ch/pops/indxhtms/gc1832en.html). UNEP set in motion the negotiation of a legally binding instrument for implementing international action on persistent organic pollutants (POPs), which is due to be signed in Stockholm, Sweden, in May 2001. The POPs instrument seeks to restrict or eliminate all uses of DDT and eleven other substances, such as dieldrin, aldrin and polychlorinated biphenyls (PCBs). Of these dozen chemicals on the POPs list, DDT is easily the most beneficial because of its role in malaria control. The other substances may not have the health benefits of DDT; however some (especially PCBs in electronic goods) are used in many developing countries. Although all the chemicals were invented in developed countries and were used extensively in the past, none of the twelve substances is still used in the countries now promoting the POPs process. This makes the ratification of the POPs treaty, in principle, politically and economically very easy for developed nations, while depriving developing countries of the chemicals that benefited the economies and welfare of the developed world. Some governments appear to be pursuing political goals through agencies such as the UNEP, and a few are attempting to achieve their goals at the expense of those at risk from malaria in developing countries (Dyson, 2000).

Five Inter-governmental Negotiating Committee (INC) meetings were held between June 1998 and December 2000 in order to agree on the final text of the POPs treaty. The fate of DDT under the POPs treaty changed dramatically during the five negotiating meetings. Initially it appeared that DDT would probably be banned for all uses.

Delegates of developing nations faced several difficulties at the INC meetings. Perhaps the most important impediment to their ability to negotiate an agreement that would have been suitable and beneficial to developing countries was that they were swamped by delegates from developed countries and representatives of environmental pressure groups.

According to the UNEP provisional list of participants to the final INC held in South Africa, the G7 countries[5] had 100 representatives between them. The environmentalist NGOs that would all have been broadly campaigning against the continued use of DDT sent 75 representatives and the European countries (including EU G7 countries) sent 87 representatives. Compare this with the total number of representatives that Sub-Saharan Africa sent, which amounted to a total of 19 excluding South Africa and 35 including South Africa. (The only reason that South Africa managed to send 16 representatives to the INC5 was because it was held in that country).

That seven highly developed countries were able to send over five times as many representatives as 17 Sub-Saharan countries

---

5   The group of seven countries (G7) is made up of the United States, Canada, United Kingdom, France, Italy, Japan and Germany.

Chart 1 **Comparison of representatives to POPs INC5 meeting**

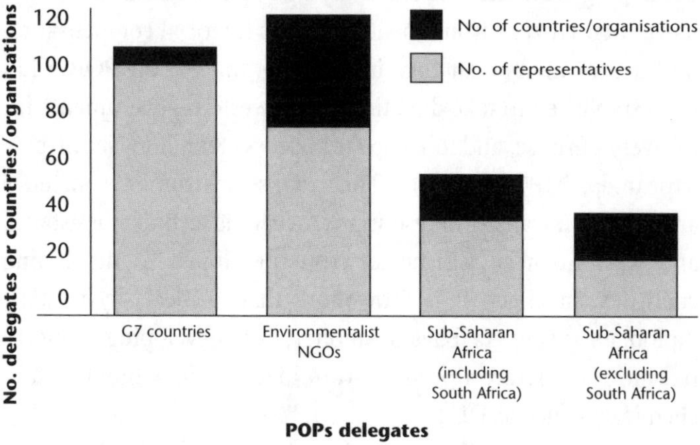

Legend:
- ■ No. of countries/organisations
- ▨ No. of representatives

X-axis (POPs delegates): G7 countries | Environmentalist NGOs | Sub-Saharan Africa (including South Africa) | Sub-Saharan Africa (excluding South Africa)

Y-axis: No. delegates or countries/organisations

Source: UNEP, 2000b.

(excluding South Africa) indicates the strength with which these nations can assert themselves by sheer weight of numbers. Most of the Sub-Saharan African countries only sent one representative to the INC meetings and they were frequently required to be in more than one negotiating room at a time, making their task almost impossible.

The country delegates to the UNEP meetings are either career bureaucrats or environmental specialists. The original representative from the WHO was an environmental specialist who did not support the use of DDT at the third negotiating session in Geneva in 1999 (see Bate, 2000). While this was understandable since the POPs instrument is essentially about restrictions of environmental pollutants, it was unnecessarily blinkered to miss the bigger picture of malaria control and development needs of poor countries. Of course, the only way that politicians from developing countries would actively sign up to policies that would harm their citizens would be if there was financial compensation (at least for the bureaucrats) in so doing. Indeed, the POPs Club was established to take donations from western governments for this very purpose, and it has so far raised $3.8 million (see http://irtpc.unep.ch/POPs_Club). The POPs instrument includes articles about transfer of resources (Article J is technical assistance and K is financial assistance) from developed to developing countries. In effect, it is little more than bribery, by western diplomats using taxpayers' money, of developing country treasuries to extract a promise from LDCs to do without certain chemicals – such as DDT.

The delegates to INC5 agreed the final text for the POPs convention and it appears that, under this mechanism, DDT will remain available to countries that require its use in disease control. DDT has been placed on Appendix B of the POPs convention, which requires its use to be restricted, rather than eliminated as with substances on Appendix A.

The text of Appendix B gives sufficient flexibility for countries to continue to use DDT on condition that equally safe, effective and affordable alternatives are not locally available. Importantly, the treaty does not specify a date by which time DDT use should be eliminated, as had been previously proposed by environmentalist groups. The way in which DDT has been treated in the POPs convention can be seen as a partial victory for those campaigning for its continued use and for countries that desperately need the insecticide. There are however certain requirements within Appendix B which could place a relatively onerous burden on developing countries.

Such requirements include regular reporting to the UNEP Secretariat and WHO on the amounts of DDT used, the conditions of such use and the relevance of such use to that Party's disease management strategy. In addition, the Parties are required to develop regulatory and other mechanisms to ensure that DDT is used only for disease control and that it is not used for agricultural or other uses. While such requirements may not be burdensome for developed countries, they will be for developing countries that face budget restrictions and lack bureaucratic capacity.

The POPs convention also requires that Parties undertake measures to strengthen health care and reduce incidences of the disease. It also requires that suitable alternatives to DDT be used as part of resistance management strategies. To have included this in the POPs convention seems unnecessary, as it is surely the aim of departments of health to improve their nations' health and to manage insecticide resistance. Indeed the continued use of DDT will reduce the incidences of disease, but should be used as part of resistance management programmes.

Environmentalism and disease control

While the final text of the POPs convention seems more accommodating to developing and malarial countries, the convention will not be able to stop the continued pressure that is applied by environmentalist groups to some of the world's poorest countries.

At the outset of the negotiations on the POPs convention, the stance of environmental pressure groups was uncompromising. They demanded the banning of DDT, which they, and their supporters, considered a 'dangerous life-threatening chemical'

(Greenpeace, 2000a). This stance changed, however, due to the inability of the environmentalist movement adequately to justify its argument, given the enormous life-saving benefits that DDT provides and the unsubstantiated and unscientific evidence of its supposed environmental and human health impacts. In addition, the final INC was held in South Africa, a developing and malarial country that indeed uses DDT to fight malaria, and it was therefore politically astute for groups such as WWF to soften their stance on DDT.

While this may have been politically astute, it is most likely to have been a temporary measure and does not preclude these organisations from campaigning against DDT outside the POPs process. Greenpeace has for some time been campaigning against Hindustan Insecticide Limited's factory in Kerala, India, one of the very few remaining producers of DDT (Greenpeace, 2000b). Given the substantial funding that Greenpeace[6] has for its anti-DDT activities it is most likely that this type of campaigning will continue to the detriment of malaria sufferers.

Liroff (2000) of the World Wildlife Fund argues that DDT should be phased out in the long term, based on the laboratory tests that suggest its potential harmful effects. Liroff supports his arguments with evidence from Mexico that indicates that the country has reduced its reliance on DDT and has substituted it with synthetic pyrethroids. The Mexican malaria control programme has used low-volume spraying techniques to lower the required amounts of insecticides and has therefore achieved cost savings. The move away from DDT in Mexico is in fact sensible

---

6   Greenpeace's total income for 1999 exceeded £19 million and it devoted over £1 million to its Toxics Campaign (Greenpeace, 2000b).

given that resistance to it has been recorded, although it still works very effectively as a mosquito repellent[7] (Rodriguez, 2000).

Mexico's achievements in malaria control and in using new technologies are commendable. However Liroff misses the vital point. Controlling malaria in Mexico is different from controlling malaria in Mozambique or in Indonesia and what works in Central America will not necessarily work in Asia. There are alternatives to DDT and indeed alternative spraying techniques, but citing Mexico as an example of what could be done elsewhere is naïve and misleading. It picks the one scientific study that supports the green case, and alleges wider application than warranted. The dogmatic green solution of 'one size fits all' is worryingly similar to the imperialist solutions of the past.

Many non-governmental organisations (such as Greenpeace and WWF), transnational organisations (such as the WHO) and donor agencies (such as USAID) are also generally against pesticide-based vector control. As all the donor agencies that operate in malarial countries and sponsor malaria programmes are from developed Northern countries, they are frequently required to follow protocols developed for their countries. For example, USAID cannot support overseas activities that are illegal in the US (Dyson, 2000). This can lead to inappropriate programmes being implemented.[8]

---

7   Widespread resistance has already been recorded to Deltamethrin, which unlike DDT does not act as an effective repellent (Rodriguez, 2000).

8   The only paper submitted by Belize to the POPs web site is about the problems of disposing of DDT from Belize (see Alegria, 1999). It explains how nearly three tons of DDT almost fell into a river (implying that Belize cannot be trusted with any synthetic chemicals of any sort), but not why that DDT had not been used for malaria control (which is why it was purchased three years previously), and was sitting unused in a poorly maintained warehouse. A possible explanation (see Dyson, 2000) is that USAID pressured Belize into not using DDT, and hence the previous importation of the powder became an embarrassment. Another

More sinister, however, is the pressure that donor agencies can and do place on the governments they are purportedly assisting to comply with their (the donor agency's) environmental and health guidelines. There are several examples of pressure placed on impoverished malarial countries by aid agencies.

In Mozambique, officials at the Department of Health have been strongly advised by its donors not to introduce DDT into the vector control programme (Mabunda, 2000; Baretto, 2000). Mozambique is one of the world's poorest countries and has been struggling to rebuild its national infrastructure and economy after a civil war that lasted nearly twenty years. Because of these circumstances, the country is heavily reliant on donor funds for the provision of even the most basic services to its population.

The use of DDT in its malaria control programme would be an attractive option because it is cheap, easy to use and highly effective. The need to use DDT is becoming increasingly urgent because of the resistance of the *Anopheles funestus*[9] mosquito to the synthetic pyrethroid pesticides.

In Mozambique, malaria control initiatives are supported by, among others, the Norwegian Development Agency (NORAD), the Swedish International Development Agency (SIDA), the Swedish Aid Agency, USAID, and UNICEF. With the exception of UNICEF, which said that it would follow the recommendations of the WHO,[10] none of these agencies supports the use of DDT in vector control (Renshaw, 2000).

---

explanation is that the DDT had become 'caked', it was unusable and therefore was awaiting disposal.

9   *Anopheles funestus* is a major and highly effective malaria vector in Southern Africa.

10 The WHO has lately recommended the use of DDT. See www.fightingmalaria. org for a letter dated 1 May from Dr Ebraham Samba, Head of WHO Africa.

NORAD discovered several years ago that funds it had donated were being used for vector control programmes using DDT. NORAD reacted by issuing a statement that it could not support policies that used pesticides or other chemicals that could not be legally used in Norway (Azedo, 2000). Similarly, SIDA has stated that it cannot support the use of DDT in any country as it was banned in Sweden in 1975.

UNICEF has implemented two malaria control strategies in Mozambique. The first is an ongoing programme that provides pesticide-impregnated bed nets[11] to communities in the Zambezia province. This programme also uses chloroquine as a 'first line of defence' drug. UNICEF started an initiative in response to flooding in Mozambique and has begun to supply 150,000 bed nets in Gaza province (Renshaw, 2000). While bed nets can be a useful element in a comprehensive malaria control programme, doubts are emerging about their effectiveness when used on their own. Recent research shows that unless the entire community has insecticide-treated bed nets and they are used effectively, they prove ineffective in malaria control (see Curtis, 1999).

While insecticide-treated bed nets offer a degree of personal protection, they are only effective in reducing overall malaria rates and in protecting whole communities when they are distributed systematically and their use is monitored – much in the same way as a spraying programme. The efficacy of bed nets varies from location to location and depends largely on cultural norms and their social acceptability (Coetzee, Hunt, 2000). Bed nets may also reduce immunity to the infection so that a child of, say, ten years old could contract the disease and die, whereas without bed nets he or

---

11   The pesticides used are synthetic pyrethroids.

she would have built up a certain immunity and would not suffer as greatly from the disease in later years (Curtis, 1999). It is possible the child would have died before reaching ten years had he not had the protection of a bed net, so it is not clear whether this argument is strong.

USAID is currently formulating its malaria control strategies in Mozambique and has stated that the policy will be 'very different' from other strategies and will include a very 'systematic approach' to the problem and will have many different interventions (Ferrara, 2000). To date, USAID has not sponsored or undertaken any vector control efforts.

Mozambique is not alone in coming under pressure from donor agencies. In Bolivia, USAID pressured the government not to use DDT in its malaria control programme and the government complied with USAID's wishes (US Govt, 1994). In Madagascar the United Nations Development Programme (UNDP) attempted to stop DDT use for malaria control and wanted the country to use Propoxur, a carbamate, instead. Despite this pressure, Madagascar, to its credit, did not change its spraying programme and continues to use DDT for malaria control. It is likely that this episode has soured the relationship between this severely impoverished country and an important donor agency. At face value, the argument that an aid agency cannot do something elsewhere that is illegal in the home country (such as condoning the use of DDT) seems reasonable. But aid agencies must often encounter conditions in recipient countries that are far removed from those of the donor country. If they really want to help they must surely be flexible enough to adapt to those conditions. For instance, would SIDA really refuse to fund hospital nurses in Africa if they work in conditions which do not fulfil Swedish health and safety requirements?

Environmental folly

The argument that using pesticides, such as DDT, is inconsistent with the goals of sustainable development and can damage the natural environment is flawed in many respects. The way in which the pesticide is used in malaria control is highly specific and well managed. Modern malaria control programmes use global positioning satellites (GPS) to pinpoint the exact locations that require spraying. The pesticide is sprayed on the inside of houses and the chance of its escaping into the wider environment is very low. In South Africa, the use of DDT has received the approval of a leading and authoritative environmental and conservation group, the Endangered Wildlife Trust (EWT). The EWT has trained pesticide sprayers so that DDT can be used with the minimum possible impact on the environment. The EWT also continuously monitors DDT use and considers that the environmental risks associated with its use are extremely low (Verdoorn, 2000).

The precautionary principle and DDT

Environmentalists often claim we should apply precaution to decisions involving chemicals. The precautionary principle is used by environmentalists to justify the restriction of certain technologies on the grounds that these technologies might be harmful. There are numerous different definitions of the precautionary principle (PP), but perhaps the most extreme is Greenpeace's: 'do not admit a substance until you have proof that it will do no harm to the environment' (cited in Morris, 2000).

However, scientific proof does not always seem to be a requirement for environmentalists. One of Greenpeace's INC5 updates contains the following statement that is nothing if not enlightening on the way in which environmentalists regard science and facts. Greenpeace states: 'If precaution had been exercised when the first evidence emerged that a chemical has potent environmental problems even in the absence of scientific certainty, much damage can [*sic*] be averted. But relying on a precautionary approach based purely on science is not good enough' (Greenpeace, 2000a).

Aside from the curious grammar, Greenpeace ignores the benefits that the chemicals it seeks to ban have brought mankind. It seems to be conveniently forgotten that DDT has saved countless millions of lives, while Greenpeace struggles to find some evidence that it harms mankind. More worrying is that it seems to suggest that precaution should not be based on science but on other criteria.

As Morris details, the PP is not only confused, but can lead to outcomes that are entirely harmful. Fundamentally the way that the PP is often interpreted fails to recognise that every activity that man undertakes involves risk of some sort and the only way to reduce risk to zero is to die. It is impossible to prove that any particular technology will not do harm to the environment as it is always possible to overlook a potential harm, even after the most thorough analysis.

Putting these objections to the PP aside however, if one were to apply the PP to DDT, the conclusion would unequivocally be in favour of its continued use and promotion.[12] Goklany argues in favour of DDT because of its great value in saving human lives and because human health and human lives must take precedence over other species. In addition, the benefits of its use are far greater

---

12   See Morris, 2000 for wide-ranging discussion of the precautionary principle.

than any supposed negative human health impacts and, because the benefits are felt immediately, while any potential negative impacts will take place in the future, DDT passes the PP test. Should environmentalists argue that the environmental impacts of DDT are irreversible,[13] one is obliged to counter that 'the death of a human being is irreversible, and more heinous than the death of a bird, for instance' (Goklany, 2000: 4).

When one considers the malaria control strategies of the past, which included pouring petroleum on breeding sites and the removal of wetlands, the responsible, indoor use of DDT is likely to have had a far lower impact on the environment. The loss of habitat for the numerous species that depend on wetlands and marshes for survival is likely to be more environmentally damaging than any of the exaggerated claims of environmental damage that have been levelled against DDT.

Sustainability for whom?

The World Wildlife Fund (see, for example, wwf-uk.org/news/news100.htm), Physicians for Social Responsibility (PSR) and the Pesticide Action Network (PAN) are some of the most vociferous campaigners for a ban on DDT. The WWF has recently acknowledged the positive role that DDT has played and continues to play in malaria control. But WWF proposes that other malaria control methods be used instead of DDT, which should be phased out. Its proposals include a general move away from reliance on pesticides towards bed nets and drug therapies

---

13   There is strong evidence to suggest that the potential impacts of DDT are reversible in any case (Goklany, 2000: 4).

and vaccines. The WWF suggests using other pesticides that it claims are as effective as DDT and are without the alleged dangers to human health and the natural environment, although these claims do not stand up to scrutiny (Grieco et al., 2000; Attaran et al., 2000).

Numerous criticisms can be made of the WWF proposals and those of PSR and PAN, which resonate with the élitism and arrogance that is so often a feature of such organisations. The logo of the WWF Toxic Chemicals Initiative reads: 'Let's leave our children a living planet.' Clearly, this emotive message suggests a responsible organisation that protects the most vulnerable. But if its plans are carried out, millions of children will not be alive to see the planet. The consequences of WWF's one-sided preoccupation are not hard to predict, but do not seem to have been considered by WWF leaders.

The proposals proffered by these environmentalists conflict directly with those of over 350 malaria scientists and physicians from around the globe, including several Nobel laureates, who have signed a letter arguing that DDT use should be actively encouraged rather than banned (see www.malaria.org). Ignoring or dismissing these calls will take a certain blinkered arrogance.

The WWF proposals, by virtue of their 'high-tech' nature, would place significant burdens on malarial countries, forcing them to be ever more reliant on donor funds. Indeed, part of the WWF proposals is for increased funding of malaria control by developed nations. Increased funding for malaria research and control is vital, but so too is the ability of sovereign nations to be able to provide lasting malaria control. A major problem with reliance on donor funds for specific programmes is that funds can be withdrawn unilaterally. Examples of this have occurred in the Gambia[14] and in Tanzania.[15] Financial sustainability is frequently overshadowed by environmental sustainability in the zeal to achieve 'sustainable development'.

In addition to the danger of donors removing funding, there is the additional problem that donors do not always act in the best interest of the recipient country. Recently agencies, such as UNICEF and the World Bank, rejected outright proposals made by the Harvard Centre for International Development (CID) that would have ensured that all donor projects be evaluated by a multi-disciplinary, transparent expert review panel. The panel would assess the scientific and operational value of proposals which, according to the Harvard CID, would improve the likelihood that donor agencies would fund successful programmes (De Gregori, 2000; Yamey, 2000; Attaran, 2000).

The WWF lists as one of its concerns that DDT destined for malaria control or some other health use could be somehow appropriated by other users such as farmers and used in agriculture (WWF, 2000). These concerns are seriously exaggerated as the quantities of DDT used in health programmes are a fraction of those that would be required if agriculture used the insecticide in any effective way. Even in countries that have not banned DDT for agriculture, such as Swaziland, the only user is the local Department of Health in its malaria control programme (Kunene, 2000). In addition, the WWF ignores the fact that DDT,

---

14   In the Gambia, the British Medical Research Council (MRC) funded a bed net programme, which collapsed after the MRC removed funding and malaria rates returned to previous levels (Coetzee, 2000).

15   In Tanzania, USAID removed funding from a bed net programme, leaving the community particularly vulnerable to malaria as the bed nets had reduced immunity to the disease (De Gregori, 2000).

and most particularly good quality DDT, is difficult to obtain – even by national departments of health (Maharaj, 2000).

The WWF is concerned that 'development and irrigation projects' are a possible source of disease outbreaks (WWF, 1998). The logic of this argument is not clear, but it seems to suggest that programmes aimed at increasing wealth and prosperity in impoverished communities are a direct contributor to ill health. That the WWF considers development and efforts to increase prosperity somehow responsible for ill health is disturbing.

6 DDT – ENVIRONMENTAL SAVIOUR?

As will be established later in the discussion of pesticide resistance (see Box 2 on p.66), DDT is cost effective and efficient in malaria control, so that large numbers of people can be protected at a very low cost. This contrasts with the significantly more expensive options of drug therapy as a malaria control strategy, the use of bed nets and more expensive pesticides such as synthetic pyrethroids or carbamates.

Opponents of DDT often fail to appreciate that ensuring that people are healthy and able to lead economically productive lives can be highly beneficial to the environment. Those suffering from malaria are anaemic and listless and are often unable to work or perform economically productive activities to the best of their ability. If an individual is unable to afford fuel such as paraffin because he has been ill with malaria, he will be forced to rely on firewood as a source of fuel. Chopping down forests and the consequent removal of natural habitats is one of the most widely recognised causes of the decline and extinction of animal and plant species. It is expensive in time and money to care for the environment. The use of cost-effective and efficient pesticides can protect the maximum number of people and allow them to lead healthy, safe and productive lives. Only when people are healthy and well fed can they afford the luxury of environmentalism (Morris & Bate, 1999).

Box 2 **The development of resistance**

The exact causes of resistance to pesticides among insects are not entirely clear. One theory is that large concentrations of an insecticide trigger a response, probably an 'ancestral response', in insects that originally evolved as a biological response mechanism to naturally occurring toxins. One of the fundamental properties of living matter is genetic variability. Those insects in which the ancestral response is triggered are likely to survive while the others are not. The development of resistant insects following exposure to insecticides derives from this basic property of selection of the fittest individuals as ancestors to the current population.

Another theory is that, in some instances, the presence of the insecticide causes a point mutation that could arise at any time. There is no substantial evidence that insecticides cause any genetic changes themselves.

Resistance could arise due to behavioural changes. For instance, insects could learn to avoid resting on surfaces that contain the insecticide as it causes irritation. While such behavioural changes may not result in any genetic changes over time, the efficacy of the insecticide in killing the insect will be reduced.

While there is no unequivocal reason for the development of resistance in mosquitoes, it is likely to be caused by a combination of factors. Obviously, the mosquito population must have the recessive genes in its population that can be selected out to confer resistance. However, the degree and method of insecticide pressure will affect the rate at which it appears. If insecticides are applied in sub-lethal doses, survivors will remain. If they breed, then the next generation is tougher, and so on.

Sub-lethal doses are likely where the DDT is not properly

applied, or where the DDT spray is not properly mixed. DDT is not soluble in water and has to be suspended with chalk or talc. Manufacturers usually guarantee the mixture for a year or so, but often it may be mixed by sprayers from the powdered DDT. It is probable that there is variation in the quality of the powder produced and even more variation in application.

Moreover, the spread of resistance comes from multiple uses of pesticides. Where anti-mosquito pesticides are also widely used in agriculture, resistance is more likely to spread rapidly. For example, the same pesticides were used in protecting cotton crops in India, Mexico, El Salvador and Guatemala as were used for spraying indoors for mosquito control and there was some increase in insecticide resistance in anopheline mosquitoes as a result (Chapin and Wasserstrom, 1983). Other examples of this phenomenon were found in growing coffee in Peru (Collins, 1988), bananas in Costa Rica (Packard and Brown, 1997) and rice in parts of Asia (Mellanby, 1992). As is explained in detail in this chapter, resistance to synthetic pyrethroids in *A. funestus* may have been encouraged by widespread agricultural use of pyrethroids in South Africa.

The largest contributor to resistance to any pesticide is intensive use over a considerable area. It selects the carriers of resistant genes and reduces the 'competition they would have suffered from the majority of normal mosquitoes' (Mellanby, 1992: 58).

Source: Hunt, 2000; Invest, 2000; Rotrosen, 2000

Considering the history of malaria control policies, it is likely that DDT is probably one of the most environmentally friendly of malaria control strategies precisely because it allows governments to provide protection and safety to enormous numbers of people at very low costs.

Pesticide resistance and the case for DDT

There is a more compelling and urgent case against the banning of DDT under the POPs Convention. In 1996, South Africa took a decision to phase out the use of DDT in its malaria control programme. There were several reasons for this move. First, there was a general international move away from the pesticide, initiated by pressure from environmental lobby groups and research funding agencies (Sharp & Le Sueur, 1996). Second, the pesticide was not always appropriate in all control situations. For example, while DDT successfully controlled the *A. arabiensis* vector, it stimulated bedbugs and other insects that were a nuisance to households. Third, the pesticide leaves a white stain on the walls. While this makes it easy for sprayers to check that the house is protected, some households re-plaster over the pesticide in order to hide the unsightly white marks, rendering it useless. Many houses in rural areas are no longer constructed with mud and dung and are made from brick, with internal walls plastered and painted. In these cases, DDT is less effective as it does not impregnate the wall (Tren, 1999). Lastly there was a concern that DDT levels in men and women in endemic areas were significantly higher than the acceptable daily intake (Sharp & Le Sueur, 1996). However, DDT toxicity in mammals is likely to be very low or negligible. Even though DDT can be passed to infants through mothers' milk, no associated toxicity has been proven. There is also no convincing evidence that DDT or its metabolites are carcinogenic to humans (Smith, 2000).

In South Africa, DDT was phased out of KwaZulu-Natal and Mpumalanga in 1996 and out of the Northern Province in 1999. Synthetic pyrethroids such as deltamethrin and cyfluthrin were used in its place. Initially these pesticides proved to be effective and had some advantages over DDT. For example, these pesticides do not increase bedbug activity and do not stain walls, making them more socially acceptable. The pesticides are also more acceptable to the environmental pressure groups and donor agencies, which would be more likely to fund their use. The South African Department of Health at the time was highly confident that the use of DDT in malaria control would never be necessary (Lombard, 1999).

There are however several disadvantages to the synthetic pyrethroids. These new pesticides were developed for agricultural use, and immediately went into widespread use. This inevitably led to vector resistance because it is impossible to guarantee the correct dosage over large areas or to prevent weak solutions escaping in run-off from fields. Therefore, some mosquitoes will come into contact with a sub-lethal dose, triggering the resistance process described above. These pesticides are also significantly more expensive than DDT and more complicated to administer. The increased cost to the already limited budgets of the provincial health departments means that fewer structures can be sprayed and fewer individuals protected.

Data for the 1997/98 spraying season show that the Northern Province in South Africa, which still used DDT, managed to spray almost seven times the number of structures as Mpumalanga Province and at a lower cost per structure (Table 1a).

A comparison of spraying costs of the various pesticides in the various locations is given below in Table 1b. The differences in the cost per structure are also affected by differences in the types of

Table 1a **Amounts and costs of insecticides for indoor spraying during 1997/98 season for Mpumalanga, Northern Province and KwaZulu-Natal, South Africa[1]**

Insecticide	Northern Province	Mpumalanga	KwaZulu-Natal
DDT			
Quantity (kg)	82,791	0	0
Cost (rand)	1,661,615	0	0
Deltamethrin			
Quantity (kg)	68	1,861	6,641
Cost (rand)	12,291	336,375	1,200,360
Cyfluthrin			
Quantity (kg)	1,350	356	0
Cost (rand)	1,389,501	366,416	0
Total number of structures sprayed	900,024	131,870	244,271
Total cost	3,063,407	702,791	1,200,360
Cost (in rand) per structure	3.4	5.3	4.9

Source: South Africa Department of Health.

structures and in the efficiency with which the sprayers use the insecticides.

Perhaps a more important problem than cost is resistance by the major malaria vectors to synthetic pyrethroids. Pyrethroid resistance has been reported in both west and east Africa by the *A. gambiae* vector, which is the major malaria vector in these parts (Hargreaves et al., 2000). In Southern Africa, resistance has been discovered in *A. funestus*, which is a highly efficient vector of the

---

1   Costs calculated as follows: 1kg DDT = R20.07, 1kg Deltamethrin = R180.75, 1kg Cyfluthrin = R1,029.26. Source: Department of Health, 1996a.

Table 1b **Comparative costs per structure and per m² of different insecticides: 1997/98 spraying season for Mpumalanga, Northern Province and KwaZulu-Natal, South Africa.**

Insecticide	Cost per structure sprayed (rand)	Cost per m^2 (cents/m^2)
DDT	2.26	5.35
Deltamethrin	3.81	7.23
Cyfluthrin	9.28	20.58

Source: South Africa Department of Health, 1996a.

disease, feeding almost exclusively on man and living in and around human structures.

A. funestus had almost disappeared from South Africa by the early 1950s, when DDT was widely used in malaria control. There was an isolated sighting of *A. funestus* in a small village near Tzaneen in the Northern Province in 1975; until recently, however, the vector had never again been seen in South Africa. *A. funestus* still remains abundant in neighbouring Mozambique.

A. funestus returned to South Africa, particularly to the KwaZulu-Natal province in the late 1990s where malaria rates have been increasing for the past few years (Table 2). The return coincided with the withdrawal of DDT from malaria control programmes and the introduction of synthetic pyrethroids (SP). As mentioned earlier, where SPs are used very extensively in agriculture, the chance that resistance will develop among mosquitoes and other insects is increased. In addition to this change, there has been higher than average rainfall in the past few years and an increase in migration of people between Mozambique and South Africa. While these and other factors have influenced the rise in malaria cases, the withdrawal of DDT and reliance upon an insecticide that *A. funestus* can tolerate is likely to be a major contributor (Coetzee, 2000).

Table 2 **Malaria cases in KwaZulu-Natal**

Year	Cases	Deaths	Change in cases %	Change in deaths %
1996	8,693	32	–	–
1997	11,425	38	31	19
1998	14,575	112	28	194
1999	27,238	214	87	91
Jan–Nov 2000	39,739	323	46	51

Source: South Africa Department of Health.

A. funestus is tolerant of synthetic pyrethroids, but it remains completely susceptible to DDT (Hargreaves et al., 2000). While there are certainly other pesticides that would be as effective as DDT in killing the vector, none can be used as cost effectively as DDT. Carbamates have been introduced to the malaria control programme in southern Mozambique as part of the Lebombo Spatial Development Initiative (SDI) and Mozal project (described below). Carbamates, such as Bendiocarb, are however 22 times more expensive than DDT in an undissolved state and 4 times more expensive once applied (see Table 3, p.73 below). This cost increase limits the scope of other malaria control activities, such as the provision of drugs, bed nets and education programmes.

DDT spraying was reintroduced into KwaZulu-Natal in March 2000. Although it is too early for scientific studies to have recorded any noticeable change in either malaria rates or the number of vectors, anecdotal evidence from malaria control staff in the province suggests that the pesticide has proved remarkably successful thus far in removing all anopheline mosquitoes (Mthembu, 2000). It is perhaps most remarkable that DDT is still the cheapest pesticide, given that it is produced by only one or two monopoly/government companies in socialist countries, such as

Table 3 **The cost of various insecticides used for adult mosquito control**

Insecticide (Wettable powders)	Concentration (g/active ingredient [a.i]/Kg)	Application rate (a.i./m²)	Cost/kg (rand)	Cost/m² (cents)
DDT	750	2	28.00	7.47
Bendiocarb	800	0.4	626.12	31.31
Cyfluthrin	100	0.02	1,623.50	32.47
Deltamethrin	50	0.02	312.00	12.48
Lambda-Cyhalothrin	100	0.031	661.92	20.52
Fenitrothion	400	1	65.36	16.34

Source: South Africa Department of Health, 2000.

India and China. Its cost would probably be far lower if it was produced by more competitive chemical companies in the west.

7 ECONOMIC COST OF MALARIA

Malaria is a human tragedy.[1] More than that, the disease imposes enormous economic costs on some of the world's poorest countries. These costs are significant enough for a well-established axiom, 'Malaria Blocks Development' (MBD), to have been developed by cultural anthropologists (Brown, 1983). Although there is an underlying anthropological concern (see Packard and Brown, 1997) about who predominantly benefits from the development[2] (historically colonial powers and latterly multinational companies are the most obvious beneficiaries), there is no doubt that malaria slows growth.

This study examines the economic costs that malaria has imposed on one particular development project in Mozambique, a country where malaria is endemic. Other economic studies that have attempted to measure the cost that malaria imposes on economies will then be examined.

---

1   For example, according to Pampana (1963), malaria infection often tragically leads to spontaneous abortions in pregnant women.

2   Early malaria control opened up land for development, but it is alleged that often the poor did not benefit from agriculture, rather the 'owners of large tea plantations' did (Packard and Brown, 1997: 188), with little or no trickle-down effect. However, it is an inescapable fact that those countries with substantial inward investment are wealthier and healthier (Goklany, 1998).

Government regeneration and the control of malaria

The Lubombo Spatial Development Initiative (SDI) is a joint initiative between the South African, Swazi and Mozambican governments. The SDI concentrates mainly on tourism and agriculture, with one of the main focal points being the Greater St Lucia Wetland Park. In addition there are four additional projects that straddle the three countries involved.[3] It is expected that over R1 billion ($142 million) will be invested in the SDI and several thousand jobs will be created (Lubombo SDI).

The SDI programme has been developed by the South African government in an attempt to 'unlock inherent economic potential in specific southern Africa locations by enhancing their attractiveness for investment. The SDI aims to facilitate potential investment opportunities, identified through the process, to be taken up by the private sector' (Lubombo Spatial Development Initiatives in Southern Africa).

Malaria and Mozal – doing good while doing well

The Mozambican government provided a number of investment incentives to the Mozal project, the most ambitious inward investment project in Mozambique's history. These included locating the Mozal aluminium smelter in an industrial free zone, which ensures that the plant is taxed at only 1% of turnover and is exempt from all customs duties, sales and circulation taxes. The government has also ensured that the plant will be able to repatriate dividends and loan repayments and is able to hold foreign exchange

---

3   These are: Hlane-Mlawula (Swaziland), Jozini-Luvamisa (SA and Swaziland), Ngumu-Thembe-Futhi (Mozambique) and Ponto do Ouro – Kozi Bay (Mozambique and SA).

offshore. The Mozambican government placed an official of the department of trade and industry (CPI) at the permanent disposal of the Mozal team in order to allow goods to be imported efficiently and to smooth the entire production process.

Part of the motivation for the Mozal project came from Eskom, the South African electricity utility, which wanted to expand some of its production outside South Africa, and Mozambique, which wanted to rebuild some of the country's damaged electricity infrastructure. Billiton plc, the London-based minerals group, saw an opportunity to utilise some of the surplus hydroelectric power generated by the Cahora Bassa dam, which was built in the early 1970s under the Portuguese administration of Mozambique (Harvard Business School, 2000). As the internal electricity infrastructure has been damaged, electricity from Cahora Bassa dam is directed through the South African grid and then Eskom supplies electricity back to Mozambique.

Mozal is a new and highly sophisticated aluminium smelter located at Matola, close to Maputo in southern Mozambique. The Mozal project is a joint venture between Billiton plc, Mitsubishi of Japan, the South African Industrial Development Corporation[4] and the Mozambican government. The first phase of the project involved an investment of $1.2 billion (projections were initially for $1.34 billion) in order to produce 250,000 tonnes of primary aluminium a year. The smelter has been designed to allow for a doubling of plant capacity to 500,000 tonnes a year, which would involve an additional investment of $800 million.

The significance of the initial investment in Mozambique is

---

4   The Industrial Development Corporation is a South African government-owned development bank with assets of $3.6 billion.

hard to overstate. According to the World Bank Development Indicators (2000), the GDP of Mozambique in 1998 was $3.9 billion, with little foreign direct investment (FDI). The Mozal investment swamped all other FDI and was a major factor in economic growth.

Billiton plc already owns and operates two aluminium smelters in the northern KwaZulu-Natal province of South Africa and has significant investments in two aluminium smelters in Brazil. The choice of Mozambique as an investment destination for a large multi-national firm is not an obvious one. Mozambique is ranked as one of the world's poorest countries and emerged from a seventeen-year war in 1992. This war was one of the most brutal and destructive in Africa and left the country with its infrastructure and economy in a state of ruination.

Aluminium smelters are very power intensive and the Mozal plant is expected to use 450 MW of power, which is double the present total power consumption of Mozambique. Eskom has constructed two power lines from South Africa to Mozambique in order to provide the power, and has agreed to link the price of electricity to the London Metals Exchange (LME) price of aluminium. This means that when the aluminium price is low, the cost of one of the major production inputs will be low and vice versa.

While labour costs and the cost of raw materials are less important factors to the operation of the aluminium smelter, these costs are lower than they would be in South Africa and significantly lower than they would be in developed countries. Labour costs, for example, are set to be around one-fifth the level that they would be in a Western-world smelter (Harvard Business School, 2000). Billiton has undertaken, in an agreement with the Mozambican government, to ensure that 90% of the smelter employees during construction and operation are Mozambicans.

Data collection initiative

One factor that the Mozal team could not plan for sufficiently was the problem of malaria. While malaria has always been endemic to Mozambique, there are very few reliable statistics on the incidence of the disease. The civil war brought all malaria control initiatives to a halt and the government has been unable to initiate a comprehensive and effective malaria control programme since then. In southern Mozambique a malaria control programme has been started as part of the SDI.

Since malaria impedes development, the SDI has started its own malaria control programme that covers South Africa, Swaziland and Mozambique. Initial studies into malaria infection rates have produced some startling results. In northern KwaZulu-Natal, the return of *A. funestus* has contributed to a sharp rise in malaria incidence from 9.5% to 40%. In this region, it should be stressed, DDT spraying was halted in 1996 and synthetic pyrethroids were used instead. Swaziland, however, has consistently used DDT in its malaria control programme and the infection rates in this country reflect the efficacy of this strategy. In Shewula in northern Swaziland on the border of Mozambique, an infection rate of 2% was measured; however at Namachanga, which is on the Mozambican side of the border and very close to Shewula, the infection rate was 40%. Infection rates in other parts of Mozambique are far higher, reaching 86% at Catuane, on the border with South Africa (MRC, 2000).

Mozal malaria costs (indirect)

Malaria has imposed significant costs on the developers of Mozal. Preliminary estimates show that direct and indirect costs of malaria to the Mozal construction team are just under R18 million (US$ 2.73 million).[5] Economic costs comprise the direct health-care costs, which include medication, testing, physician time in treating the disease and vector control and education costs. Indirect costs are made up of the cost of lost productivity while workers are incapacitated due to the disease. The cost calculations include all the malaria cases from the inception of the project until 10 June 2000. All the cost data have been collected from the Mozal on-site clinic, which is the first consultation point for all on-site malaria cases. There are some malaria cases that will not be captured by the clinic as certain employees will develop the disease while off-site and will report to a different clinic and receive treatment elsewhere. These economic costs should therefore be viewed as a conservative estimate.

All workers are entitled to five days of sick leave, even if they are no longer incapacitated after three days. In general, expatriate employees will normally be incapacitated for between five and seven days, while local employees will be incapacitated for between three and five days. For the purposes of calculating the economic costs, it is assumed that expatriates are unable to work for six days and local employees are unable to work for five days. This does not take into account that malaria sufferers will most likely feel enervated and listless for some time after they have taken five or six days off work and that productivity will therefore be lower than normal.

---

5   The combined totals of Tables 4 and 5.

The cost of lost productivity accounts for the bulk of the economic cost of malaria, at over R5 million (US$ 726,000) or 28% of the total costs shown in Tables 4 and 5.[6] This assumes that the hourly wage of local workers is around R5.00 and that for expatriate workers is R28.13 (Maire, 2000). The disparity in the wage rates is because Mozambican wage rates are in general lower than those in South Africa and also because expatriate workers will generally be more skilled.

Mozal malaria costs (direct)

All employees at the Mozal site are treated with the same drug regimes. For mild cases, Fansidar is used, while for more complicated cases quinine is administered. In some cases quinine has to be administered intravenously if the patient is unable to take the medication orally. It is estimated that approximately 60% of cases are treated with Fansidar, 30% require oral quinine treatment and the remaining 10% require IV quinine (du Plessis, 2000). Drug costs are estimated to be in the order of R640,000 (US$ 91,000) or about 3% of the total economic cost.

Testing for malaria also accounts for approximately 3% of the total economic cost of the disease. A malaria slide test is performed between two and three times per malaria episode and costs R22.41 per test. A rapid malaria test is sometimes performed on those cases that arrive at the Mozal clinic after normal hours. No records are available on the number of rapid tests that are performed and they have therefore been excluded from the calcula-

---

6   This figure ignores the cost of those who are sick for longer than six days and subnormal performance immediately after returning to work.

tions. All cases also receive glucose rapid tests and haemoglobin rapid tests in addition to the malaria slide tests. Each case receives two such tests and they cost R7.91 and R4.25 per test respectively. The total cost of malaria tests (Table 4) is about R600,000 (US$ 85,000).

Very serious, complicated cases of malaria are evacuated to medical centres in South Africa, which imposes a significant cost. Over the construction period between July 1998 and June 2000, a total of 90 cases were evacuated by air and 248 cases were evacuated by road. There is no record of where these cases were taken within South Africa, but it is likely that the majority were taken to Nelspruit, the nearest city in South Africa to Maputo. Some cases will have been evacuated to Johannesburg or Durban, which would involve significantly higher costs of transport.

Even though air evacuations are normally reserved only for the most serious of malaria cases, they are sometimes undertaken for less serious cases. This is because road evacuations frequently are hampered by uncooperative customs officials on the Mozambican side and poor road conditions in Mozambique (Castle, 2000).

On average, air evacuations from Maputo to Nelspruit cost R9,000 while road evacuations for serious cases cost marginally less at R8,000 (Castle, 2000). It is assumed that all air evacuations use fixed-wing aircraft and that the road evacuations require life-support equipment in the ambulances. On the basis of these costs, the evacuation of malaria cases has cost the project developers in excess of R2.7 million (US$ 385,000), as shown in Table 4, or 15% of the total economic cost.

In addition to the evacuation costs, there will be costs of hospitalising patients and the nursing and physician costs. It is expected that nurses on average will spend half an hour with each malaria patient, while physicians will spend up to three-quarters of an hour (du Plessis, 2000). The hourly rate of nurses and physicians varies from hospital to hospital: however the South African Medical Association (SAMA) standard rate for physicians is R300 ($43) per hour.[7] Nursing rates vary widely depending on the number of years of experience and qualifications: an hourly rate has been estimated at R200 ($28; Millpark Hospital, 2000).

The majority of the malaria patients do not require hospitalisation and are treated at home. Those cases that are evacuated, however, will require hospitalisation and would be treated in private clinics in South Africa. The non-medical hospitalisation costs, such as food and laundry, are R590.60 per patient per day on a medical ward (Hospital Association of South Africa). Some malaria cases will require treatment in an intensive care ward, but these data were not available and it is therefore assumed that all patients are admitted to a general medical ward. The additional hospitalisation costs therefore are of the order of R1.2 million (US$ 171,000), or 7.5% of total costs.

Mozal vector control

Mozal has implemented a comprehensive vector control programme in and around the smelter site, the costs of which are shown in Table 5 on p.85. The vector control programme includes the spraying of structures with synthetic pyrethroid insecticides, the supply of bed nets to staff, larviciding any potential breeding pools and an education and awareness campaign.

Insecticide spraying has occurred at the smelter site itself and

---

7   This is based on the medical insurance rate for reimbursement.

Table 4 **Summary of non-vector control economic costs of malaria:
Mozal project**

Item	Cost (in rand)	% of total
Indirect costs		
Productivity costs	5,082,550	41
Direct costs		
Malaria tests	595,167	5
Evacuation costs	2,794,000	22
Drug costs	640,349	5
Physician/Nurse time	2,122,577	17
Hospital costs	1,197,737	10
Total	12,432,380	100

Source: Authors' estimates.

within a 1.6 kilometre buffer zone. The spraying is coupled with
a monitoring programme that assesses the number of anopheline
mosquitoes within the area. An ultra-low-volume, high-pressure
sprayer ensures that the spray reaches some normally inaccessi-
ble areas such as ceilings that are at a height of approximately 30
metres. The spraying programme has proved remarkably successful within the buffer zone. During February and March (the
months when mosquitoes are most active) 2000, the monitoring
programme found approximately sixty anopheline mosquitoes
per structure outside the buffer zone. Within the 1.6 kilometre
buffer zone, the number of malaria vectors fell to only five and
no malaria vectors were found within the smelter site itself
(Kloke, 2000).

In addition to the spraying programme at the smelter site and
within the buffer zone, Mozal has contributed US$ 580,000 to the
Lubombo SDI malaria control programme. This contribution has
enabled the SDI to extend the spraying area up to the smelter site,
rather than just within the SDI area. It is expected that Mozal will

have to make an additional contribution to the SDI malaria programme in order to cover the additional costs incurred in purchasing carbamate pesticides. While the additional contribution has not been finalised, it is likely to be in the order of US$ 200,000 (van den Bergh, 2000). These extra funds could have been applied to other health projects if DDT had been used.

The emergence of *A. funestus* resistant to synthetic pyrethroids is hampering the malaria control efforts and it has therefore been necessary to introduce carbamates as an alternative insecticide. Initial reports suggest that resistance is also developing to the carbamate insecticides, which could further destabilise the malaria control programme (Coetzee, 2000; Kloke, 2000). Carbamates have an additional problem in that they are highly effective in exterminating cockroaches, crickets and other insects living in and around dwellings and these insects are then eaten by ducks and other poultry. The high dose of carbamates that is then ingested by ducks frequently proves fatal, which makes the spraying programme unpopular with householders. While these social and environmental problems can be addressed by ensuring that all insects are cleared away and poultry locked up during spraying, the issue of resistance cannot be dealt with as simply (Maharaj, 2000).[8]

---

8 Resistance management has been more successful at the Hillside plant in South Africa, where there is a choice of several pesticides. As South Africa can afford its own health budget, it has made the decision to allow DDT use for vector control. There is also the more prosaic advantage that the low cost of DDT means a larger area can be protected.

Table 5 **Vector control and education costs for Mozal and SDI (in rand)**

Contribution to SDI spraying initiative	3,360,000
Mozal vector spraying	840,000
Education, training and bed nets	1,050,000
Total	5,250,000

Source: van den Bergh, 2000.

Opportunity costs of malaria

The direct and indirect costs of malaria, described above, are considerable and would be at least partially avoidable if a comprehensive and effective malaria control strategy were in place in Mozambique. In addition to these costs are the opportunity costs imposed by the disease. The Mozal developers have already expressed reservations about expanding capacity of the plant because of the malaria problem (Barbour, 2000). Of great concern to Mozal is that they will not be able to attract the required professional expatriate staff to the smelter. Given that at least ten expatriate employees have died from malaria since construction of the plant began[9] and almost 3,300 expatriate cases have been recorded, these concerns should not be underestimated. The expansion is expected to involve an investment of approximately US$ 800 million and would provide desperately needed income and employment opportunities to Mozambique.

A major facet of the Lubombo SDI is tourism and the current malaria epidemic could prove a serious hindrance to tourism development in South Africa and Mozambique. The Lubombo SDI is well placed to develop the tourism industry given the wide range and extent of the local natural resources. There are numerous

---

9   As at 10 June 2000.

national parks, private game reserves, coastal reserves and a range of other tourist activities. But should tourists feel unsafe, they are unlikely to be attracted to the area. Given the myriad alternative tourist destinations in Southern Africa, the malaria threat to the Lubombo SDI is very significant. It is noteworthy that many resorts in Southern Africa specifically and prominently promote the fact that they are in non-malarial areas, which is a partial indication of the seriousness with which tourists view malaria.

8   WIDER ECONOMIC COSTS

Tren (1999) estimates that malaria costs selected Southern African countries[1] approximately US$1 billion in direct health costs and productivity costs. It should be noted that these estimates are conservative and do not consider the wider opportunity costs nor the impact that malaria has on cognitive development in children and the ability of countries and regions to develop.

While the majority of malarial countries are poor, the causal relationship between poverty and malaria is not an obvious one. It is not immediately clear whether the disease causes countries to be poor, or whether it is poverty that results in high malaria rates. Gallup and Sachs found that annual growth rates between 1965 and 1990 in countries that suffer from severe malaria were between 1% and 1.3% lower than they would have expected without malaria (see Table 6 on p.88). This takes into account factors such as the initial poverty of the countries, the tropical location of the countries and overall life expectancy. Those countries that reduced their malaria rate by 10% showed a 0.3% rise in annual economic growth. Gallup and Sachs conclude that malaria is an important determinant of poverty and the continued presence of malaria ensures that malarial countries will remain poor (Gallup & Sachs, 2001). Their estimates of the economic growth penalty,

---

1   South Africa, Swaziland, Tanzania, Namibia, Zimbabwe, Zambia.

Table 6 **Loss of economic growth in 31 malaria-endemic African countries, 1980–95**

Country	Aggregate loss (millions of PPP-adjusted 1987 $)	Per person loss (PPP-adjusted 1987 $)	As a fraction of actual 1995 income
Benin	1172	214	18%
Botswana	503	347	5%
Burkina Faso	1684	162	18%
Burundi	730	117	18%
Cameroon	4227	318	18%
Central African Republic	884	270	18%
Chad	995	154	17%
Congo	759	288	18%
Congo, Dem. Rep.	7125	162	18%
Cote d'Ivoire	4107	294	18%
Gabon	1389	1290	17%
Gambia	251	226	18%
Ghana	5355	314	18%
Guinea Bissau	152	142	14%
Kenya	5272	198	18%
Lesotho	0	0	0%
Madagascar	2280	167	18%
Malawi	1072	110	18%
Mali	1222	125	17%
Mauritania	611	269	15%
Mauritius	0	0	0%
Namibia	832	539	10%
Niger	1457	161	17%
Nigeria	17,315	156	18%
Rwanda	656	102	18%
Senegal	2426	286	18%
Sierra Leone	366	87	17%
South Africa	4056	98	1%
Togo	1166	285	18%
Zambia	1359	151	18%
Zimbabwe	4214	383	18%
Total	73,638	185	10%

Source: Based on results in John Luke Gallup and Jeffrey D. Sachs, 'The Economic Burden of Malaria' in *Economics of Malaria* (2001).

in terms of loss of income, are in Table 6.

The figures are reported in purchasing power parity (PPP) adjusted dollars held constant at 1987 prices. This corrects for the effects of price inflation, as well as the fact that, in Africa, non-traded goods and services (for example, health services or land) are cheaper relative to internationally traded goods than they are in the United States. In order to convert these units into current US dollar terms, it would be necessary to divide by a factor of about 3, then multiply by the rate of price inflation between 1987 and 1995.

There are many factors that such economic analysis cannot take adequately into account, such as the cognitive impairment of children that suffer from malaria and the full extent of lost productivity of those who care for malaria victims. The cost of a reduction in economic growth rates of 1% per annum (1965–98) is estimated at $100 billion for Africa (in 1998 prices). In other words, had malaria been eradicated in 1965, Africa's GDP would have been about 40% higher by 1998 (Gallup and Sachs, 2001).

Restricting economic development is especially problematic environmentally as well as in terms of human well-being. This is particularly the case in developing countries because richer is cleaner, healthier, longer-lived and less susceptible to adversity (Goklany, 1995a, 1995b, 1999, 2000a, 2000b). As Goklany has noted, economic development is not an end in itself, but it provides the means for numerous ends. Virtually every indicator of human well-being improves with the level of economic development (Goklany, 1999, 2000a, 2000c). Economic development creates wealth and helps increase food supplies per capita, which reduces malnutrition. Because economic development reduces malnutrition and hunger as well as making basic public health services more available, it reduces mortality rates and increases life expectancies (see Figure 1, Goklany, 2000b). Also, total fertility rates (a critical determinant of birth rates) drop with increasing rates of economic growth (Goklany, 2000c). For each of these indicators of human well-being, improvements are most rapid at the lowest levels of economic development (Figure 1, Goklany, 2000b, 2000c).

9 CONCLUSION

Malaria has plagued mankind for countless generations. It inhibits development, causes untold suffering and illness and claims millions of lives every year. The one-weapon war against malaria eradication, ostensibly controlled by WHO and funded and led primarily by USAID, unravelled in the 1960s. Failure to achieve eradication, environmental concern encouraged by Rachel Carson's ideological adherents, and increasing acceptance of the neo-Malthusian message of over-population, all contributed to the demise of DDT use. The US stopped funding the WHO's special eradication account between 1961 and 1963. USAID switched funding from anti-malaria programmes to family planning programmes, and shifted responsibility for malaria to the US Public Health Service, as though it disowned its previous efforts (Packard, 1997).

USAID deserves credit for saving tens of millions of lives by funding DDT use. Its failure to achieve eradication (although perhaps inevitable) led it to turn its back on DDT and, eventually, all forms of insecticidal spraying. While this is perhaps understandable, its recent actions of denying funding to those who want to use DDT again are objectionable. The critics of USAID activities in the post-war years have been joined by modern critics who bemoan the 'one size fits all' cultural model of health (see Packard and Brown, 1997). A centralised, narrowly focused attack is still being made on malaria, while ignoring local conditions and concerns. Today it is bed nets and medicines, where previously it was DDT.[1] It appears that political control by these agencies will only countenance a single approach at a time. According to Baird (1999), alternatives to vector control are essential in Africa, where the disease is endemic and malaria-carrying mosquitoes proliferate in so many parts. However, in parts of Asia and South America, vector control is still the most effective weapon because malarial areas are smaller and often eradication or significant control of mosquito populations is possible. So not only is the focus on bed nets and drugs misguided for Africa, but it is even less applicable outside Africa (Baird, 1999).

WHO's critics complain that modern-day efforts to control malaria also ignore the issue of poverty. They often deplore (albeit tacitly) efforts by companies like Billiton to protect their staff, because it creates a stark disparity between them and the surrounding communities who are 'excluded' from the protected area. They compare this with the governmental authorities of the past in places like Rhodesia (now Zimbabwe) (Packard, 1997). Of course, the objection does not stand up for long if properly aired: is it not better to protect as many people as possible, even if some are not helped?

Health agencies in developing countries and working companies like Billiton are at least trying to stem the resurgent malarial tide. They require a large arsenal of weapons to fight malaria, and with the spreading *A. funestus* resistance to synthetic pyrethroids, the requirement for DDT is stronger than it has been for thirty years.

---

1   Similarly, from the 1940s to the 1970s most research money was spent on new insecticidal discovery, whereas today most is spent on drugs and vaccines.

It seems clear that the outcome of the UNEP POPs Convention negotiations will make it possible for those countries that need DDT to continue to use it. That the country delegates arrived at this compromise is commendable, particularly given the strength and power of those campaigning for the elimination of DDT. It is most likely, however, that environmentalist groups and donor agencies will not relent from their crusade against DDT. Vigilance will be needed to ensure that the world's poorest countries are not continuously disadvantaged in an ongoing anti-DDT campaign, having already won a partial victory under the POPs convention.

Malaria kills a few million every year. Each life lost is a potential Mandela, Shakespeare or Edison, and nothing is less reversible than death, nor more tragic than the death of a child. Hundreds of millions suffer chronic illness, which creates a painful economic burden and perpetuates poverty. This may not be the intention of those who propose a DDT ban, but it surely will be the outcome.

REFERENCES

Alegria (1999) Web publication, <http://www.chem.unep.ch/pops/pops%5Finc/proceedings/cartagena/alegria.h17/08/00>

Attaran, A., Roberts, D., Curtis, C., Kilama, W. (2000), 'Balancing risks on the backs of the poor', *Nature Medicine* 6(7): 729–731 July.

Attaran, A. (2000), 'Promises once, promises twice: a view on the Abuja Declaration and a new opportunity for African malaria control', *Harvard CID*, Cambridge, USA.

Azedo, A.-H. (2000), Norwegian Development Agency (NORAD), Maputo Office, personal communication, 26 May 2000.

Barreto, A. (2000), Deputy National Health Director, Head of Department of Epidemiology and Endemics, Ministry of Health, Mozambique, personal communication, 24 May 2000.

Baird, J. K. (1999), 'Resurgent Malaria at the Millennium: Control Strategies in Crisis, Parasitic Diseases Program', Working Paper, *US Naval Medical Research Unit*, No. 2.

Barbour, R. (2000), Chairman Mozal, personal communication, 8 May 2000.

Bate, R. (2000), 'A New Kind of Health Club', *Wall Street Journal Europe*, 15 May 2000.

Brown, P. J. (1992), 'Socioeconomic and Demographic Effects of Disease Control: The Case of Malaria Eradication in Sardinia',

Medical Anthropology 7:63–87.

Brown, P. J. (1997), 'Malaria, *Miseria*, and Underpopulation in Sardinia: The Malaria Blocks Development Model', *Medical Anthropology* 17, 3: 239–254.

Bruce-Chwatt, L. J. & de Zulueta, J. (1980), *The Rise and Fall of Malaria in Europe: a historico-epidemiological study*, Oxford University Press.

Butler, E. (2000), Director, Avima Pty Ltd, personal communication, 3 July 2000.

Carlson, D. G. (1984), *African Fever. A Study of British Science, Technology and Politics in West Africa, 1787–1864*, Watson Publishing International, Canton, USA.

Carlsson, L. (2000), Swedish International Development Agency (SIDA), Maputo Office, personal communication, 31 May 2000.

Castle, M. (2000), Medical Rescue International, Nelspruit, personal communication, 1 July 2000.

Chapin, G. & Wasserstrom, R. (1983), 'Pesticide use and Malaria resurgence in Central America and India', *Social Science and Medicine* 17: 272–290.

Coetzee, M. & Hunt, R. (1993), 'African Anopheline Mosquito Taxonomy and the Control of Malaria', in *Entomologist Extraordinary, Botha de Meillon*, ed. Maureen Coetzee, Department of Medical Entomology, South African Institute for Medical Research, Johannesburg.

Coetzee, M. (2000), Head, Department of Medical Entomology, South African Institute for Medical Research, personal communication, 18 May 2000.

Collins, J. (1988), *Unseasonal Migrations: The Effects of Rural Labor Scarcity in Peru*, Princeton University Press, Princeton.

Commonwealth Secretariat (2000), 'Commonwealth African Region Workshop on Integrating Economic and Environmental Policies and Using Economic Instruments to Promote Environmentally Sustainable Development, Background Material', Commonwealth Secretariat, London.

Creamer, T. (1998), 'Anti-malaria plan opens way for jobs in Lubombo', *Engineering News*, 13 November 1998.

Croumbie Brown, J. (1890), *African Fever and Culture of the Blue Gum-Tree to Counteract Malaria in Italy*, W. & W. Lindsay, Aberdeen.

Curtis, C. (1999), 'Malaria Control: bednets or spraying? Background and trial in Tanzania', *Transactions of the Royal Society of Tropical Medicine and Hygiene* 93: 453–454.

De Gregori, T. (1999), 'It Has Been a Very Good Century, But', *Priorities For Long Life and Good Health* 11(3): 7–11, 40.

De Gregori, T. (2000), 'Let Us Spray: Malaria and DDT in Mozambique', drkoop.com online and ACSH.com online

Desowitz, R. S. (1993), *The Malaria Capers: Tales of parasites and people*, Norton, New York.

du Plessis, L. (2000), Carewell Management International, personal communication, 10 May 2000.

Dyson, J. (2000), 'Why we must think again about DDT', *Reader's Digest*, October 2000.

Ferrara, P. (2000), Director, USAID, Mozambique Office, personal communication, 2 June 2000.

Gallup, J. L. & Sachs, J. D. (2001) 'The Economic Burden of Malaria', *Centre for International Development at Harvard*, October 2001.

Gell-Mann, M. (1994), *The Quark and the Jaguar*, Little, Brown and Co., London.

Goklany, I. M. (1995a), 'Strategies to Enhance Adaptability: Technological Change, Economic Growth and Free Trade', *Climatic Change* 30: 427–449.

Goklany, I. M. (1995b), 'Richer is Cleaner: Long Term Trends in Global Air Quality', in: R. Bailey (ed.), *The True State of the Planet* (New York, NY: The Free Press), pp. 339–377.

Goklany, I. M. (1999), 'The Future of the Industrial System', invited paper, International Conference on Industrial Ecology and Sustainability, University of Technology of Troyes, Troyes, France, 22–25 September 1999.

Goklany, I. M. (2000a), 'Potential Consequences of Increasing Atmospheric CO_2 Concentration Compared to Other Environmental Problems', *Technology* 7S: 189–213.

Goklany, I. M. (2000b), 'Applying the Precautionary Principle to Global Warming', Center for the Study of American Business, Washington University, St. Louis, Mo., USA Policy Study (forthcoming).

Goklany, I. M. (2000c), 'Economic Growth and Human Well-being', Political Economy Research Center (PERC), Working paper.

Goklany, I. M. (2000d), 'Applying the Precautionary Principle to DDT, Global Warming, and Genetically Modified Crops', in *Rethinking Risk and the Precautionary Principle*, Julian Morris (ed.), Butterworth Heinemann, Oxford.

Greenpeace (2000a), 'Analysis . . . Paralysis, Late edition. POPs negotiations: Musings of a common man, the return!', web publication, <http://www.greenpeace.org/%7Etoxics/html/content/popinc_dec8.html>

Greenpeace (2000b), 'Greenpeace Annual Report 1999', web publication, <http://www.greenpeace.org/report99/index.html>

Grieco, J. P., Achee, N., Andre, R., Roberts, D. (2000), 'A Comparison of House Entering and Exiting Behavior of Anopheles vestitipennis (Diptera: Culicidae) Using Experimental Huts Sprayed with DDT or Deltamethrin in the Southern district of Toledo, Belize', *Journal of Vector Ecology*, 25; 1: 62–73.

Hall, J. (2000), SNC-Lavalin EMS Mozal Construction Services, personal communication, 10 May 2000.

Hargreaves, K. K., Koekemore, L. L., Brooke, B. D., Hunt, R. H., Mthembu, J., Coetzee, M. (2000), 'Anopheles funestus resistant to pyrethroid insecticides in South Africa', *Medical and Veterinary Entomology* 14: 181–189.

Harrison, G. (1978), *Mosquitoes, Malaria and Man: A History of the Hostilities Since 1880*, John Murray, London.

Harvard Business School (2000), 'Financing the Mozal Project', 9-200-005, *Harvard Business School*, Harvard.

Harvard Centre for International Development, 'The Case for a Vaccine Purchase Fund', Harvard CID web publication, <http://www.cid.harvard.edu/cidmalaria/malaria.htm>

Hlophe, N. (1999), 'Lubombo SDI on tract to raise R1billion', *Business Report*, Johannesburg, 26 February 1999.

Hoare, C. (1998), 'Ambitious KwaZulu-Natal programme: Southern Africa united in the fight against Malaria', *Mercury Newspaper*, Durban, 24 June 1998.

Hunt, R. (2000), Department of Medical Entomology, South African Institute of Medical Research, personal communication, 18 May 2000.

International Conference (1937), 'Report of the League of Nations Intergovernmental Conference of Far-Eastern Countries on Rural Hygiene', Bandoeng.

Kloke, G. (2000), Malaria Control Officer, Mozal, personal communication, 10 May 2000.

Kmietowicz, Z. (2000), 'Control malaria to help defeat poverty, says WHO', *British Medical Journal*, BMJ 2000; 320: 1161 (29 April 2000).

Kunene, S. (2000), Head of Malaria Control, Swaziland Department of Health, personal communication, 26 June 2000.

Invest, John (2000), Head of Vector Control, Aventis plc, personal communication, 25 May 2000.

The Lancet (2000), 'Donor responsibilities in rolling back malaria', Editorial, *The Lancet*, Volume 356, Number 9229, 12 August 2000.

Liroff, R. (2000), 'Reduction and elimination of DDT should proceed slowly', Commentary, *British Medical Journal*, Volume 321, pp. 1404–1405, 2 December 2000.

Litsios, S. (1997), ' Malaria Control, the Cold War, and the Postwar Reorganization of International Assistance', *Medical Anthropology* 17, 3: 255–278.

Le Sueur, D., Sharp, B., Appleton, C. (1993), 'Historical perspective of the malaria problem in Natal with emphasis on the period 1928–1932', *South African Journal of Science*, Vol. 89, pp. 232–239.

Lombard, D. (1999), Director, Communicable Disease Control, Vector Borne Diseases, National Department of Health, personal communication, 8 April 1999.

Longstrup, E. (2000), Director, Danish International Donor Agency (DANIDA), Maputo Office, personal communication, 26 May 2000.

Lubombo Spatial Development Initiative, 'Overview, Key Projects', LSDI web publication, <http://www.sdi.org.za/

Profiles/lubombo.html

Mabunda, S., Dr. (2000), Malaria Programme, Department of Epidemiology and Endemics, Ministry of Health, Mozambique, personal communication, 24 May 2000.

Mack-Smith, D. (1959), 'Italy: A Modern History', University of Chicago Press, Chicago.

Maharaj, R. (2000), Director, Communicable Disease Control, Vector Borne Diseases, National Department of Health, personal communication, 10 July 2000.

Maire, N. (2000), Mozal, personal communication, 7 June 2000.

Malkin, M., and Fumento, M. (1999), 'Rachel's Folly: The End of Chlorine' in Mooney, L. and Bate, R. (eds.), *Environmental Health: Third World Problems First World Preoccupations*, Butterworth Heinemann, Oxford.

Mansell Prothero, R. (1965), *Migrants and Malaria*, Longman, London.

Martin, C. (1998), 'World Wildlife Fund, Feature Story – Handling Technology With Care', WWF web publication, <http://www.panda.org/news/features/07-98/story5.htm>

McCarthy, D., Wolf, H., Yi Wu (1999), 'The Growth Costs of Malaria', Mimeo Georgetown University.

Mellanby, K. (1992), 'The DDT Story', The British Crop Protection Council, Surrey, UK.

Millpark Hospital (2000), Human Resources Department, personal communication, 1 July 2000.

Missiroli, A. (1949), 'L'Influenza della Scomparsa della Malaria sulle Condizione Sociali ed Economiche dell'Italia del Sud', *Rivista di Parassitologia* (10): 271–272.

Morris, J. & Bate, R. (1999), *Fearing Food: Risk, Health and Environment*, Butterworth Heinemann, Oxford.

Morris, J. (2000), *Rethinking Risk and the Precautionary Principle*, Butterworth Heinemann, Oxford.

Mthembu, J. (2000), Malaria Programme, Department of Health, KwaZulu-Natal, personal communication, 26 June 2000.

National Academy of Sciences (USA NAS) 2000, *'Proceedings'*, 97, 1: 331–336.

Nosten, F., van Vugt, M., Price, R., Luxemburger, C., Thway, K. L., Brockman, A., McGready, R., ter Kuile, F., Looaressuwan, S., White, N. J. (2000), 'Effects of artesunate-mefloquine combination on incidence of Plasmodium falciparum malaria and mefloquine resistance in western Thailand: a prospective study', *The Lancet*, Volume 356, Number 9226, pp. 297–302, 22 July 2000.

Packard, R. M. (1997), 'Malaria Dreams: Postwar Visions of Health and Development in the Third World', *Medical Anthropology* 17, 3: 279–296.

Packard, R. M. & Jones, P. (1997), 'Rethinking Health, Development and Malaria: Historicizing a Cultural Model in International Health', *Medical Anthropology* 17, 3: 181–194.

Packard, R. M. & Gadehla, P. (1997), 'A Land Filled with Mosquitoes: Fred L. Soper, the Rockefeller Foundation and the Anopheles Gambiae Invasion of Brazil', *Medical Anthropology* 17, 3: 215–238.

Padden, Thomas (2000), Former EPA offical 1971–9, personal communication, 6 October 2000.

Prins, E. (2000), South African Medical Association, personal communication, 29 July 2000.

Reiter, P. (2000), 'From Shakespeare to Defoe: Malaria in England in the Little Ice Age', *Emerging Infectious Diseases* 6: 1, Centers for Disease Control and Prevention.

Renshaw, M. (2000), Malaria Director, UNICEF, Mozambique, personal communication, 31 May 2000.

Roberts, D. R., Manguin, S., Mouchet, J. (2000), 'DDT house spraying and re-emerging malaria', *The Lancet*, Volume 356, Number 9226, pp. 330–332, 22 July 2000.

Roberts, D. R. (2000), personal communication, 12 December 2000.

Rodriguez, M. H. (2000), Centro de Investigaciones sobre Enfermedades Infecciosas, Instituto Nacional de Salud Pública, Mexico, personal communication, 15 December 2000.

Rotrosen, S. (2000), former Chairman of Montrose Chemical Ltd, personal communication, 30 June 2000.

Sharp, B. & le Seuer, D. (1996), 'Malaria in South Africa – the past, the present and selected implications for the future', *South African Medical Journal*, Volume 86, No.1, pp. 83–89.

Silva, K. Tudor (1997), ' "Public Health" for Whose Benefit? Multiple Discourses on Malaria in Sri Lanka', *Medical Anthropology* 17, 3: 195–214.

Slabberts, S. (2000), Hospital Association of South Africa, personal communication, 29 July 2000.

Smith, A.G. (2000), 'How toxic is DDT?', *The Lancet*, Volume 356, Number 9226, pp. 267–268, 22 July 2000.

South African Department of Health (1996a), 'Guidelines for Vector Surveillance and Vector Control', *National Department of Health*, Pretoria.

South African Department of Health (1996b), 'Guidelines for the Treatment of Malaria', *National Department of Health*, Pretoria.

South African Department of Health (1996c), 'Guidelines for the

Prophylaxis of Malaria', *National Department of Health*, Pretoria.

South African Department of Health (1997), 'Overview of Malaria Control in South Africa', *National Department of Health*, Pretoria.

South African Department of Health (2000), 'Malaria Statistics', *Communicable Diseases Control, National Department of Health*, 14 August 2000, Pretoria.

Spielman, A. (1980), 'Environmental Health Impact of the Mahaweli Development Program of Sri Lanka: Vector Borne Disease. A Report Submitted to the Government of Sri Lanka'.

Tren, R. (1999), 'The Economic Costs of Malaria in South Africa – Malaria Control and the DDT Issue', Institute of Economic Affairs, London.

United Nations Environment Programme (POPs) (2000a), Submission by South Africa: 'DDT specific exemptions and use; DDT entry and control for Annex B', 24 March 2000, Bonn.

United Nations Environment Programme (POPs) (2000b), 'Provisional List of Participants, INC5'.

United States Government (1994), Memorandum. Subject: USAID Litigation Document Search, 23 September 1994.

van den Bergh, A. (2000), Billiton plc, personal communication, 8 May 2000.

van Wyk, P. (1984), 'Field Guide to the Trees of the Kruger National Park', Struik Publishers, Cape Town.

Verdoorn, G. H., Dr (2000), Director, Poisons Working Group, Endangered Wildlife Trust, personal communication, 26 June 2000.

Vogt, W. (1949), *The Road to Survival*, Victor Gollancz Ltd, London.

Wigglesworth, V. B. (1936), 'Malaria in Ceylon', *Asiatic Review* 32: 611–619.

World Health Organization (1955), 'Malaria Eradication', Proposal by the Director General to the Eighth World Assembly, 3 May 1955. A8/P&B/10.

World Health Organization (1998), 'Roll Back Malaria. A global partnership', WHO, Geneva.

World Wildlife Fund (1998), 'Three Decades after *Silent Spring*, DDT Still Menacing the Environment', WWF press release, web publication, <http://www.panda.org/news/press/news_219.htm>

World Wildlife Fund (1999), 'Resolving the DDT Dilemma: Protecting Biodiversity and Human Health', WWF, web publication.

World Wildlife Fund (2000), 'Toxic Chemicals Initiative – Persistent Organic Pollutants', WWF web publication, <http://www.panda.org/toxics/areas_pops.cfm>

World Wildlife Fund (2000), 'UNEP Global POPs Treaty – INC4/Bonn. Eliminating DDT and Protecting Public Health', March 2000, WWF web publication.

Yamey, G. (2000), 'Donors reject screening panel for malaria projects', *British Medical Journal*, BMJ 2000; 321: 194, 22 July 2000.

ABOUT THE IEA

The Institute is a research and educational charity (No. CC 235 351), limited by guarantee. Its mission is to improve understanding of the fundamental institutions of a free society with particular reference to the role of markets in solving economic and social problems.

The IEA achieves its mission by:

- a high quality publishing programme
- conferences, seminars, lectures and other events
- outreach to school and college students
- brokering media introductions and appearances

The IEA, which was established in 1955 by the late Sir Antony Fisher, is an educational charity, not a political organisation. It is independent of any political party or group and does not carry on activities intended to affect support for any political party or candidate in any election or referendum, or at any other time. It is financed by sales of publications, conference fees and voluntary donations.

In addition to its main series of publications the IEA also publishes a quarterly journal, *Economic Affairs*, and has two specialist programmes – Environment and Technology, and Education.

The IEA is aided in its work by a distinguished international Academic Advisory Council and an eminent panel of Honorary Fellows. Together with other academics, they review prospective IEA publications, their comments being passed on anonymously to authors. All IEA papers are therefore subject to the same rigorous independent refereeing process as used by leading academic journals.

IEA publications enjoy widespread classroom use and course adoptions in schools and universities. They are also sold throughout the world and often translated/reprinted.

Since 1974 the IEA has helped to create a world-wide network of 100 similar institutions in over 70 countries. They are all independent but share the IEA's mission.

Views expressed in the IEA's publications are those of the authors, not those of the Institute (which has no corporate view), its Managing Trustees, Academic Advisory Council members or senior staff.

Members of the Institute's Academic Advisory Council, Honorary Fellows, Trustees and Staff are listed on the following page.

The Institute gratefully acknowledges financial support for its publications programme and other work from a generous benefaction by the late Alec and Beryl Warren.

The Institute of Economic Affairs
2 Lord North Street, Westminster, London SW1P 3LB
Tel: 020 7799 8900
Fax: 020 7799 2137
Email: iea@iea.org.uk
Internet: iea.org.uk

Other papers recently published by the IEA include:

WHO, What and Why?
Transnational Government, Legitimacy and the World Health Organization
Roger Scruton
Occasional Paper 113
ISBN 0 255 36487 3

The World Turned Rightside Up
A New Trading Agenda for the Age of Globalisation
John C. Hulsman
Occasional Paper 114
ISBN 0 255 36495 4

The Representation of Business in English Literature
Introduced and edited by Arthur Pollard
Readings 53
ISBN 0 255 36491 1

Anti-Liberalism 2000
The Rise of New Millennium Collectivism
David Henderson
Occasional Paper 115
ISBN 0 255 36497 0

Capitalism, Morality and Markets
Brian Griffiths, Robert A. Sirico, Norman Barry and Frank Field
Readings 54
ISBN 0 255 36496 2

A Conversation with Harris and Seldon
Ralph Harris and Arthur Seldon
Occasional Paper 116
ISBN 0 255 36498 9

To order copies of currently available IEA papers, or to enquire about availability, please contact:

Lavis Marketing
73 Lime Walk
Oxford OX3 7AD

Tel: 01865 767575
Fax: 01865 750079
Email: orders@lavismarketing.co.uk